Searching for Home

Simran Chawla was born and raised in Virginia, and has a journalism degree from George Washington University and a postgraduate degree from City University London. After working with the National Geographic Society in her early career, she now works at King's College London. Her writing about the Indian immigrant experience has appeared in magazines like *Washingtonian* and *Elle*.

Simran lives near London with her husband. This is her second book.

Searching for Home

Stories of Indians Living Abroad

SIMRAN CHAWLA

hachette
INDIA

First published in 2018 by Hachette India
(Registered name: Hachette Book Publishing India Pvt. Ltd)
An Hachette UK company
www.hachetteindia.com

SRD

ISBN 978-93-5195-074-5

Hachette Book Publishing India Pvt. Ltd
4th/5th Floors, Corporate Centre,
Sector 44, Gurugram 122003, India

Typeset in Bembo Std 11/15.9
by InoSoft Systems Noida

Printed and bound in India by
Manipal Technologies Limited, Manipal

MIX
Paper from
responsible sources
FSC® C043100

For Prit
*Anywhere in the world,
with you, I am home.*

CONTENTS

CONTENTS

INTRODUCTION

The idea for this book was born one night at a dinner party in London.

Just married and new to the city, I was introduced to a petite young woman, the wife of a good friend of my husband's. Of a cheerful disposition, Preety's shock of black curls bounced as she chatted animatedly, her hands fluttering to drive home a point. Her melodic accent was one I simply couldn't place.

'It's French,' she explained, twirling a finger around the rim of a glass of water. 'I learned to speak French before English.' Her lyrical voice and diction revealed a unique cocktail of accents: French, British and even Gujarati, the mother tongue of her parents.

'Everyone speaks French in Madagascar,' she elaborated. 'That's where I'm from.'

I could see why our respective husbands had introduced us to each other.

Like me, a person of Indian heritage who had recently married a British Indian and moved to London from my home near Washington, DC, Preety had married and moved here from Madagascar. Instantly connecting over our marriage-related migrations, we laughed together, commiserating with each other over the generally dismal local weather and our endless commutes on the Underground. I shared with her my curiosity about the Indian population in London and just how unfathomably large it seemed to be.

'There are many Indians in Madagascar too,' she acknowledged.

'In Madagascar?'

I shouldn't have been surprised to hear that, but I was.

I knew the Indian diaspora comprised large communities of Indians living across the world – in the United Kingdom, the Gulf, North America and East African countries like Kenya and Tanzania and earlier, in Uganda. But I had never heard of an Indian community in Madagascar. That Indians had chosen to relocate there made perfect sense when you looked at a map, but for someone with very little knowledge of Madagascar, it seemed as random a destination as Charleston in the American state of West Virginia, where my own family had originally moved from New Delhi.

I've always entertained a romantic notion of the path my parents' lives must have followed as they emigrated in their twenties from India to America. While their circumstances were not unique – the 1960s and '70s were a time of great Indian emigrations to America – for me, their life as a young couple unfolds like an adventure. I cannot help but admire their spirit, living as they did in an era predating the Internet and the setting up of global networks that have ironed out the hitches of travel and made staying connected a nearly effortless and trouble-free endeavour. In my eyes, they were truly courageous to leave their families behind and set forth on a journey into the unknown with the earnest desire of creating a new life in a foreign country. It almost makes me wonder: what were they thinking?

My own emigration from America to the United Kingdom after getting married is still something I'm getting used to, even after nearly eight years. I still struggle with my feelings at the airport when I'm leaving after a visit to my parents' home. I smile and exchange jokes with them as we prolong our goodbyes as close to airport security as is allowed, then cry as I go down the escalator, out of their range of vision. Before we part, my dad tries to bring a smile to my face.

'*Beta*,' he says with a grin, '*pahaunch kay khath bhej dena* [send me a letter once you've reached home.]'

I can't imagine how my parents managed to leave their homes with such limited means of communication available at the time, sending handwritten messages to their families on sheets of blue airmail which would take 15 days or more to travel from one home to another.

In America, I would often hear stories about how my parents' generation had arrived in the country a few decades ago. Living as I did in England, however, where connections with India are far more tangible and complex, and relationships with the rest of the world certainly more immediate, I was gradually exposed to the vast diversity of voyages out of India. I heard countless stories from friends, casually related over meals, about how families had come to settle in England. But it was Preety's family history, in particular, following the trajectory of their lives as they moved out from India to England via Madagascar, that captured my imagination.

That history is poised on one pivotal story, the details of which are vague. But the narrative, passed down through the years from one family member to the next, begins in India. In the mid-1900s, Preety's grandfather had set off from his village in Gujarat to find work, earn a living and make a new life in Kenya, aiming to follow in the footsteps of the many young men from his village who had already done so. He had packed his belongings and left his family home. At a dock in Mumbai (then Bombay), he boarded a ship headed towards Kenya, where he would meet relatives awaiting his arrival. After weeks of sailing, Preety's grandfather set foot on land again. He searched the port for his relatives and, having failed to find a single familiar face, began asking the locals for help. When he shared the names and address of his relatives with them, one of the locals broke the news to him.

'You are in Madagascar, not Kenya,' he was told.

'My grandfather never intended to move from India to Madagascar,' says Preety. 'He ended up there by accident.'

Whether he boarded the wrong ship or the captain of the vessel decided to change course midway remains a mystery. But Madagascar is where he landed.

With no money to return home to India or set sail on a ship to Kenya, Preety's grandfather began looking for work on the tropical island. He made a modest home for himself and, after some time, set up a business, importing and selling television sets and other electronic gadgets in Madagascar. His first marriage was to a daughter of the only other Indian family living on the island. She passed away while giving birth to their sixth child and he would later return to Gujarat to marry again. The woman he chose to be his second wife would become Preety's grandmother. He brought her back to the island, along with family members and others from his village who were keen on settling in Madagascar.

Decades later, with his business thriving, Preety's grandfather became a pillar of the Gujarati Hindu community on the island. Travelling to London on vacation to visit family members, he was inspired enough to favour a British education and lifestyle for his children and grandchildren. At the height of his fortunes, he invested his earnings in London's real estate.

In Madagascar, Preety's family lived in a large house in Antananarivo, the country's capital. 'I had a really comfortable life in Madagascar,' Preety recalls. 'But it became unsafe.'

Racial tensions, aggravated by economic disparity between the natives and the island's affluent Indians settlers, meant that crime, especially carjackings and kidnappings, was a part of life in Madagascar.

'We travelled with an escort of bodyguards and our houses had doors and windows barricaded by iron bars to keep out intruders.'

When daily life became too dangerous, Preety's family decided to leave for India.

'My parents now split their time between a house in Gujarat and England, where my sisters and I live,' she told me.

Preety's story, with its global connections through migration and marriage and her parents' eventual return to India, is a compelling one and symbolic of how the simple dream of 'moving abroad' can often become so very complicated along the way. When her grandfather set off from Indian shores all those years ago, it is possible that he never anticipated the decisions he would, one day, arrive at as he navigated a new life abroad. And surely, he couldn't have known that, one day, he would accept and build a life in a country where he had never intended to settle.

The story of Preety's grandfather goes back almost a century, but it is just as relevant today. Thousands of people leave India every year in search of opportunities abroad, just as they have done for centuries. In days gone by, Indian merchants had used the ancient Silk Road to travel and trade across China and the Middle East. Later, under the British Raj, they would travel with the Imperial Army to provide civil services across the colonial empire. Migration scholars have classified the Indian diaspora on a generational basis. The first category comprises 'old migrants' of the early nineteenth century, who were sent out of India by its British rulers as indentured labour to Malaysia (then Malaya), Mauritius, the Caribbean and British colonies in Africa. The second consists of 'later migrants', who were sent as labour to rebuild nations following the destruction and devastation wrought by the two World Wars. The third covers the 'newest migrants' of the twenty-first century, the highly skilled workforce recruited by North America, the United Kingdom and Australia.

Today, there are over 25 million non-resident Indians (NRIs) in the world. According to the Ministry of Indian Overseas Affairs, the Indian expatriate population is the second-largest in the world after the Chinese overseas community; and Indians who moved abroad have settled in almost every habitable corner of the planet.

Technically, the term 'NRI' is one that describes the tax status of a person of Indian origin. Anyone who has lived outside India for more than 182 days of the year is defined as a 'non-resident Indian'. But 'NRI' has come to mean so much more. For some, it has become a coveted label, associated with status, power, prestige and the validation that they have made a better life for themselves outside India than would have been possible in their country of origin. The halo associated with being an NRI has created a certain desperation in some to leave their country at any cost and strike out for unknown destinations. In fact, in the course of the many interviews I carried out for this book, my subjects would often describe the motivation for moving abroad as a 'craze to leave India'. Intrigued, I was driven to unearth the roots of this 'craze', which then became one of my primary reasons for writing this book.

While undertaking research for this book, I discovered Indian communities all over the world. There were many I wished to visit in person, but simply couldn't – the community across the Caribbean which dominates the medical sector; communities in East Africa or in Cape Town where, for generations, Indians have lived and worked; the communities of East Asia in Singapore, China, Bali and other countries. But my funding was limited and so I restricted my travels to places where I was able to establish personal connections.

In the end, I found myself interviewing mostly Punjabi families, partly because they represented an aspect of Indian culture I was most familiar with, but also because the stories of migration out of Punjab are predominant. Some scholars[1] trace the beginning of the Punjabi emigration out of India to the British annexation of Punjab in 1849, when Punjabi men were inducted en masse into the British Indian Army and stationed in distant lands across the Empire. Those among them who weren't absorbed into the Army were recruited for service in East Africa as civil servants and builders of the East African Railway. With the fall of the British Empire, the men of Punjab were recruited again as labourers to rebuild Britain following World War II. This critical period in the history of modern migration out of Punjab lies, perhaps, at the root of the 'craze' to emigrate, for soldiers returning to their villages in Punjab with tales of adventure in Europe and other countries would inspire their brethren to follow in their footsteps.

Whether this adequately explains the early history of the obsession to move abroad or not, it certainly seems to offer some historical basis for the current pattern, especially for the Punjab region, where young men, in particular, are seeking lives outside India. A 2012 report by the European University Institute states that every year, more than 20,000 people from the Indian state of Punjab alone attempt to migrate abroad *without* proper legal documents.[2] Nearly half that number set out to enter the European Union illegally. They travel across a complicated network of routes on their journeys to Europe – some via Russia, others through Libya, Turkey, Greece or Tunisia. They arrange for and pay thousands of pounds or euros to facilitators for the privilege of being smuggled into Europe in lorries, tankers and boats; some even set out on foot, walking great distances for days on end. Many have been apprehended at airports and seaports and one group was even caught while trekking through the French Alps to get to the next destination on its planned route. Peru, Mexico and Guatemala are the points through which undocumented immigrants are trafficked into America. Not all have made it to their final destination alive. Some have drowned, others have been murdered along the way and a few couldn't survive the gruelling journey.

Yet, every year, thousands more keep trying.

Of course, not all the narratives of emigration to overseas destinations are quite so dramatic or depressing. And, certainly, the cases of emigrating illegally are far fewer than the many thousands who emigrate to other countries legally, find the success they are seeking abroad, and contribute vastly to economies and societies of their adopted country.

Whether life is truly 'better' for Indians living in places other than their country of origin is a perception that has been defined as much by Indian pop culture as by those who left for what they considered greener pastures and by the kind of money they sent back to their families at home. Financial success often tends to eclipse the emotional anguish, cultural alienation and struggle for social acceptance that people face when they leave their familiar milieus to settle in an alien one. Visits to India by these NRIs only reinforce the notion among those living in India that life abroad is easier and rich with financial rewards.

The question arises: does money alone drive people to leave their country for foreign shores? In an age when India is one of the strongest emerging markets in the world and a potential superpower, what drives so many Indians to seek their fortunes beyond its shores? What are they aspiring for – or escaping from? How are they travelling and where in the world are they finally settling? How are their present-day experiences as 'global citizens' similar to and different from the stories of those who migrated decades or even centuries before them? These were some of the questions that drove my research for this book.

Everyone I interviewed had a common expectation on leaving India: that they would find a better life abroad. Some were able to find what they were looking for. Others were not so fortunate. Through the process of delving into their lives and thoughts, I came to know in greater detail the many reasons that had motivated them to leave for foreign climes.

The issue of corruption in India and lack of accountability on the government's part came up several times in conversation. Some declared that it was the desire 'to lead a clean life', without having to fork out bribes at every turn or go 'around the system' for daily necessities that had impelled them to seek a life elsewhere. Competition was another factor that came up in discussions. Yes, there were good universities and promising jobs on offer in India, but the competition was so cut-throat that even getting a foot in the door was difficult. The quest for bridging the class divide, along with a desire for employment security, guarantee of accommodation and greater access to healthcare and education were other motivating factors.

More personal reasons involved attempts to break away from the restrictions imposed by family and society. There were also those for whom making a life elsewhere was a way of striving for independence and earning respect. While I understood the compulsions of those seeking adventure and new horizons abroad, I was intrigued by the reasons that impelled some to risk injury and even death so that they could fulfil their dream of starting from scratch in an unknown land. I could not help enquiring of the survivors if they truly believed that what they had ultimately achieved was worth the heartbreak of leaving behind their familiar world and enduring the immense hardships involved in crossing over and establishing themselves anew.

For some, the answer was an unequivocal affirmative. Life abroad had provided them opportunities to advance and achieve their financial goals in ways that wouldn't have been possible in India. But for others, the answer was less clear. A surprisingly large number of the people I spoke to shared very similar experiences. I heard stories of how many of them had chosen to move abroad with the intention of working there for a few years before returning home to India. But inevitably, they had got so caught up in their new lives that the months had turned into years and the years into decades, without them ever looking back. Their temporary stay had somehow acquired permanence as careers, children, mortgages and a new way of life had taken over. So many of the people I met had achieved financial success and acquired social status that were truly worthy of our admiration, but it was what they had to leave behind that remained a source of perennial heartache for them: ageing and often ailing parents, empty homes and a language that now sat uneasy on their tongues and was steadily fading from their consciousness.

This book is about the modern Indian diaspora – the children and grandchildren of India who are living in cities, towns and villages across the world. They are separated by geography, but connected by common challenges – finding a home, getting a job, learning an unfamiliar language, raising children to understand and cope with dual realities – and, more significantly, by a shared nostalgia for the home they left behind. Salman Rushdie describes this nostalgia as the 'India of the mind'. It's the India my father holds on to, the India that he hasn't visited in over 30 years. This nostalgia is poised on the duality of eagerly going abroad to pursue opportunities that lie outside India, while simultaneously suffering the pangs of having wrenched oneself away from one's roots. While the appeal of life abroad shows no signs of abating, the aim of this book is to reveal that the well-trodden path to that coveted goal is not always easy, and that at each new milestone, the seeker of success in distant lands will be impelled into making decisions that may take him further and further away from his original dream.

By sharing personal narratives, I hope to offer the reader a new range of characters living abroad. Looking beyond the headlines of power achievers abroad who are CEOs of Google or Pepsi, multimillionaire business owners or the idealized 'model minorities' of the West, I hope to share valuable insights into the real lives of Indian immigrants across the world and highlight crucial issues involving the vast number of people who, by their willingness to move across countries illegally, are increasingly becoming the target of human traffickers and exposing themselves to inherent dangers. I am equally keen to share the less sensational stories, like that of the Indian families living in Italy who keep the local dairy farms alive in the countryside; of the Indian community in Alaska that built a temple to a Hindu deity on its own; or of the new generation of Indians abroad who take pride in their ethnicity and make every effort to keep their culture alive, despite the vast geographical distance that separates them from their roots.

The way contemporary Indians living abroad stay connected with their families in today's hyper-globalized world has not escaped my notice, but in no way have I sought to classify them as stereotypes or generalize their narratives, aiming, rather, to present them in terms of their individual relevance.

To lend a personal dimension to what has become a social phenomenon, I have included my own story of emigrating from America to the UK and explored my conflicted feelings about 'settling abroad'.

I am hopeful that through my efforts to understand the journey of migration, beginning with the basic expectations that inspire many to set out for the unknown and glean valuable insights from the experiences of the individuals I have met and profiled in this book, I have managed to convey some idea of the vastness of the Indian population living outside the country and the extent to which geography has shaped their experiences abroad.

I hope that I am able to convey to the reader that Indian immigrants are, above all, human beings, and as eager as any one of us to realize their potential and make a worthy life for themselves and their families. Travelling overseas to seek their fortunes is merely the perceived means to that end.

Traditionally, the ties that bind immigrants to their homeland slacken with time, but this is far from true as far as the Indian diaspora is concerned. Indian culture – covering the country's diverse languages, cuisines, festivals and faiths – has travelled down the generations and across continents with migrants, much as if it had been carried along in a big, sturdy suitcase. While its enduring strength has kept its social customs and religious practices alive for centuries within the country itself, today, that very culture also binds the dispersed offspring of immigrants to each other and to a land that lies thousands of miles away. Indians leaving their country for what they considered greener pastures, without sacrificing their loyalty to their heritage, present a fascinating paradox that was evident across the many communities I visited.

They say you can discover what people value most from observing what they carry with them when they travel. The many Indians who have left the subcontinent and continue to set out for other shores have taken with them the language, religious practices, cultural rituals and recipes of their homeland. But, perhaps, the most precious possession they carry in their hearts to their new home is the idea of India.

Notes

[1] Axel, Brian Keith (ed.), *From the Margins: Historical Anthropology and its Futures*, Duke University Press Books, 2002.
[2] Saha, K.C., *Irregular Migration from India to the EU: Punjab and Haryana case study*, CARIM – India Project, 2012.

London, England

THE HOME THAT WASN'T

Pleased with my purchases, I headed back to the car after a shopping trip in Southall, London. The car park at the Broadway is always chock-a-block with frenzied shoppers, and only after expertly manoeuvring your car across tightly packed spiralled levels can you find a parking space. My husband and I almost always park on the rooftop level. From there, we have a view of the town below us, while above us is a constant flow of aerial traffic – planes arriving and departing from the nearby Heathrow airport.

Weighed down by heavy shopping bags in both hands, I approached our car with a sigh of relief and satisfaction. After all, in just a few, short hours, I had managed to find myself two outfits to wear to an upcoming family wedding. I opened the boot and was gently laying the outfits out flat to prevent them from creasing, when I sensed a man approaching from behind. Startled, I spun around to face him. As our eyes met, he joined his palms together, his expression one of abject misery, then held his hands out to me in a plea for help.

'Please, *behenji*,' he implored in Hindi, 'please help me! I have nothing.'

His face creased, his eyes welling up as he repeated his words and spread his palms out in a gesture of helplessness.

I dug into my purse, but came up empty-handed. I had no cash left after my shopping spree.

'I'm sorry,' I told him apologetically and got into the car.

As I pulled away, I remember the man standing there motionless, his features sagging in an expression of helplessness. Tears streamed down his cheeks. He looked utterly lost, defeated. I'm always moved when I see someone in a similar predicament, but when a man of your father's generation pleads for help in the language spoken by your parents, it's simply heartrending. Deep down, I knew his was not an isolated case; he was not the only homeless Indian begging for help in Southall.

A chill grey sky presses down on London. On this drizzling, dripping Tuesday morning in the crowded borough of Southall, 31-year-old Kamaljeet aches to return home to India. With a file of neatly organized papers tucked beneath his black puffer vest, he steps into the *gurdwara*, a Sikh temple on Park Avenue that sits across the road from what once was an Asian pub called Glassy Junction.

It's that time of day when the *gurdwara* is crowded with the very old and the very young. Toddlers struggle to keep their head coverings from slipping, tottering around on unsteady legs in the vast open spaces of the durbar hall, before being scooped up into their mothers' arms and asked to bow their heads before the Sikh holy book. A sleepy, silver-bearded man sits on the floor, his back against the wall, his hands resting on his bent knees. He flicks a smile at a curious child who skips about, stares at him and waves. The air is heavy with the aroma of buttery sweet *prashaad,* a sacred offering to all who visit, as prayers are recited in a soft murmur at the front of the room. Bathed in the pale steel light of these gentle morning hours, the *gurdwara* is quiet and in the prayer hall, there is peace.

Outside the main hall, on one side of the entrance doors to the temple, grandmothers stifle their laughter. On the other, grandfathers read newspapers printed in Punjabi. As devotees enter the building, they remove their shoes and line them up on many-tiered shelves that reach the ceiling. Food supplies are dropped off in the kitchen to provide for the temple's on-going *langar* service. There is chatter everywhere and as Kamaljeet threads his way towards the staircase, everyone seems oblivious to the 'Help Desk' set up on the second floor.

In February 2010, the United Sikhs, a United Nations-affiliated organization, set up a makeshift office in an unused storage space on the second floor of the *gurdwara.* It was they who launched the 'Help Desk' programme to assist men and women like Kamaljeet who were in dire need of medical attention, accommodation or immigration advice. Every Tuesday, from ten in the morning until one in the afternoon, United Sikhs volunteer staff – that includes women like Harbans Kaur and Neelu Kaur – are stationed there to familiarize themselves with the plight of UK-based illegal immigrants from India by lending a patient ear to their stories of distress.

Many of those migrants, often uneducated and poorly informed, have been cheated by 'agents' who charged them thousands of pounds to travel to the UK. All they received in return was a set of fake documents and hellish travel conditions. Urged by those very same 'agents' to destroy evidence of their travels to make deportation more difficult if they were caught by the authorities, they have burned their valid passports and authentic documents. Now penniless, jobless and with no official immigration documentation to speak of, these men and women have been robbed of their very identity and left without the means of returning to their families in India. Many have nothing to return to, anyway, having sold everything they owned before setting out. Some were warned by their families to not return home at all unless they did well for themselves. Given the hopelessness of their circumstances, some have already fallen into a cycle of alcohol and drug abuse.

'We set up in Southall because this is where the biggest problem is,' Neelu had informed me when I visited the Help Desk one Tuesday morning back in 2013.

In fact, that Help Desk in Southall proved so successful that the model has been rolled out nationally. In the many *gurdwara*s I've visited in and around London, I've seen signs marking out similar immigration-advice hubs. Like churches, *gurdwara*s serve

22

not only as a place of worship, but as a critical community resource. With Southall targeted as a major destination for Asian migration, the number of cases handled by the Help Desk had skyrocketed during the first few years of the period beginning from 2010, when migration issues like Kamaljeet's were rampant in the area. What makes the Help Desk different from other similar services is the close collaboration between the staff and the UK Border Agency (UKBA) as they work to help men and women living in the country illegally to return home to India of their own volition.

For the most desperate among them who are living in Southall, Neelu is a welcome sight with her face brightened by a shade of lipstick that perfectly matches her magenta head covering. She and her colleague, Harbans, have been exposed to a range of immigration issues by being personally involved with dozens of cases in the area. The two work together and seem to have a stellar partnership – Neelu takes a firm and direct approach, giving honest advice, while Harbans speaks softly and sympathizes with the predicament of those who approach her.

Since the Help Desk programme was first launched, the duo has seen it all. They've helped women who had taken up prostitution to fund their journeys back to India and wives who were brought from India and had silently endured domestic abuse, not knowing to whom they could turn for help in a foreign country where they knew no one other than their marital family. They've worked with men of all ages, from the very young to the very old, to help them return to their families in India. Today, the two women are hearing out Kamaljeet and trying to help him.

He has come to the Help Desk to be voluntarily deported to India. He sits anxiously across Neelu and Harbans and shuffles through paperwork, scribbling notes as they assess his situation.

'Do you have your original birth certificate?' Harbans asks in an understanding, motherly voice, adjusting her sea-green head covering.

'No, not in England.'

'What about a passport?'

'I only have my fake passport.'

To remain in England, Kamaljeet will need to apply for legal residence in the country; to fly back to India, he'll need to show evidence that he is a person of Indian origin. Without original and authentic documentation to support either option, Kamaljeet may find himself trapped in a legal no-man's land, making him persona non grata in both countries.

His predicament is far from unique. In fact, there are similar immigration cases all across the UK, including in areas like Southall.

For over a hundred years, Southall has been a popular destination for Asian migration into the UK. I've visited it often enough to understand that on the face of it, the area, with its abundance of Indian restaurants, shops and places of worship, would seem like a familiar and reassuring destination for someone like Kamaljeet, who came to the UK with dreams of earning a fortune.

While Southall's history dates back to the early eleventh century, it is only in the past 50 years that it has become a hub of diversity. Back in the 1920s and '30s, the area used to be home to a large number of Welsh migrants who had made their way to London in search of work opportunities but, in the 1950s, it would become a coveted destination for South Asians. While popular accounts of how South Asians came to dominate the area lack precise details, it is generally believed that the influx of this community began when an Englishman, a former commander in the British Indian Army in Punjab, returned home and began working as a civil servant. He recruited men from Punjab to help in the construction work for railway projects, including the Southall railway station. Where Punjabi Sikh men in their role as soldiers in the British Imperial Army were once seen as 'protectors of the Empire', they came to be known after Independence as 'rebuilders of the Empire', engaged in repair and reconstruction work in the UK following the devastation wrought by World War II[1]. With some of the Punjabi migrant workers settling in Southall, their families from India eventually joined them. Over the years, the Asian segment of the area's population continued to grow. Today, the majority of the population in the area is of Asian descent and includes, apart from Indians, Pakistanis, Bangladeshis and a growing number of Afghans.

Posters of blue-skinned divinities promoting Indian cable television channels are plastered on the tanned brick walls of Southall's railway station. The station is perched on a hilltop and from its entrance, the view splits into two.

To the left of the station lies '*purana*' Southall or Old Southall, where merchants like Kuldeep S. Sura have sold classical Indian musical instruments like sitars, tablas and bamboo flutes for over 30 years.

'Tablas and harmoniums are the most popular,' he tells me.

Grocers like Mr Singh quietly arrange mini food bazaars on the footpaths outside their shops. 'A case of mangos for £5', reads one sign. The streets seem tinted in vintage, like a sleepy grandfather who still wears his favourite brown wool suit from the 1960s. Everything looks worn in Old Southall, except for the white and gold contours of the relatively new *gurdwara* on Havelock Road – one of the largest Sikh temples outside India. Even the traffic slows down in the narrow lanes that run past these towering domes.

To the right of the station lies Southall's bubbly younger sibling, the one loaded with one too many accessories and who occasionally has lipstick on her teeth. Weddings are big business on this side of the station. Clothing stores all along the Broadway are bursting at the seams – traditional beaded gowns and jewellery spill out onto the street. Young couples with accents picked up from various corners of the country crowd these streets to have bespoke wedding ensembles designed for them.

'The pink stones on his outfit need to match my outfit, yeah?' says one bride-to-be.

On the main high street, the Suman Marriage Bureau advertises itself as the UK's oldest Asian matchmaking service. A branch of the Indian National Bank sits right at the street corner. Punjabi and Bollywood beats blare from DVD stores and peckish shoppers queue up at street stalls to buy sweet corn sprinkled with *chaat masala* for £1.

With its station signage – 'Welcome to Southall' in both English and Punjabi – it's easy to forget that the place is a mere ten miles from central London. The India connection is visible on every street, in every alley. It isn't difficult to understand why, for people like Kamaljeet who don't speak fluent English, Southall offers a kind of comfort zone in an alien country with the sights and smells, the language, cuisine and culture of their homeland – India.

Mornings in Southall are hushed. The murmur of gentle prayers from India's range of spiritual beliefs washes over individual stores during the quiet hours before crowds of shoppers descend on the area. Supermarket workers at Quality Foods silently stock the aisles with pickled lemons and rosewater, coconut scrapers and spice grinders, lotus seeds and curry leaves. Packaged teas from Darjeeling and Kashmir sit on shelves in the aisle next to cornflakes and marmite. Older women with aching knees head for the supermarket in the morning, hunkering down to sniff at each vegetable individually before adding it to their baskets. It's still too early for children's voices to ring out on the high street.

With dozens of shops and rows of restaurants buzzing with activity in the old and new areas of Southall, commerce is thriving here, resulting in a continuous demand for workers on these streets. The character of Indian clothes is such that almost every outfit is moulded perfectly to the wearer's contours and tailors and seamstresses offer high-value services for low prices, not realizing that the silks and sewing they customize in this way could well be considered 'couture'. Troops of cooks and wait staff across the area churn out the most popular flavours for which Indian cuisine is known, making Southall 'unbeatable for Punjabi and south Indian food', according to the food column published in the *Guardian*[2]. And what about the bling? At one of Southall's gold-jewellery hubs, a handwritten sign on an A4-size sheet announces in letters written with a black marker: 'Experienced gemmologist needed'.

But not all who live in Southall need apply.

In recent years, the area has become less synonymous with the jolly backdrop of the locally filmed 2002 hit movie, *Bend It like Beckham*, than with a darker side – of illegal migrants like Kamaljeet who struggle to find employment. Poorly educated and often originating from India's rural areas, there are dozens of such illegal immigrants living here in abject poverty.

Southall's Asian population is predominantly Punjabi. A 2012 United Nations report on illegal migration indicates that every year, more than 20,000 youths from the state of Punjab alone, most of them men, attempt to move abroad illegally. Nearly half of them aim to undertake the journey to Europe, while more than a quarter aspire to make it to the UK, particularly to areas like Southall. A more recent migration report published in 2016 by the University of Oxford reveals that citizens of Asian countries account for the largest number of enforced removals and departures from the UK, with Indian nationals topping the list[3]. Motivated by the ambition of finding a job that will enable them to earn enough to financially support their families back in India, these migrants risk their lives and the little money they have to make it to London the hard way – without valid visas and legal documentation.

For some, daybreak in Southall signals a time to prepare for the long hours of business that lie ahead. For others, morning encounters determine the value of a day's work. Near the King's Street car park, known as '*kala chowk*' or 'dark street', groups of men gather every morning to vie for casual day-labour opportunities, mostly involving construction, cleaning or floor jobs in factories.

Migrant workers like Kamaljeet who have lived in Southall for years remember how, just a few years ago, daily-labour opportunities were plentiful and cash-in-hand jobs could bring in nearly £300 per week. But with the decade's economic downturn and more stringent enforcement measures implemented by the UKBA to curb immigration, such jobs are now few and far between. As a result, undocumented migrant workers like Kamaljeet have had little work in recent years. Local employers like Southall's restaurant owners and shopkeepers are now less likely to hire anyone who has entered the country illegally, fearing the hefty financial penalty – up to £10,000 per worker, according to the UKBA – they would invite if they got caught. For the jobs that do come along, the wages offered can be far below the national minimum wage – that's if such under-the-radar employees get paid at all, given their inability to seek legal redress. It comes as no surprise that Southall's migrant workers are regularly exploited, often, ironically, by '*apne*', a Punjabi word that means 'one's own people'. In this case, Indians with bona fide identity papers who are already established in the country and have no qualms about exploiting vulnerable migrant workers hiding from the authorities.

Unable to find a job and earn a daily wage, Kamaljeet is ready to return home. If only he can.

At the Help Desk, he impatiently asks for the second time, 'How soon can I go back?'

'Don't get your hopes up.' Neelu gives it to him straight. 'The soonest will be in four weeks and that's only if you can arrange all your paperwork.'

Neelu and Harbans caution Kamaljeet that if he is unable to provide any valid documents to prove his country of birth, he's likely to share the same fate as Ranjeet Singh, a migrant worker from India who had entered England illegally more than a decade ago and now exists in a legal limbo: no country will claim him as one of their own and he has no legitimate documents to establish his identity.

'He spends his life volunteering at the *gurdwara*,' Harbans says. 'You'll see him here often.'

While fumbling through his papers in search of any form of documentation that could be helpful in sending him back home, Kamaljeet begins to open up and unravel his story.

'I am an illegal,' he says in Punjabi, slumping back in his chair. 'I wanted to come to England to establish myself. I wanted to be somebody.'

Kamaljeet had turned twenty-four in 2006, the year he was smuggled into the UK after paying an agent in India to arrange for his travel to London by any available means. Against the sum he was made to fork out, he was given a counterfeit passport that he used to enter Europe.

'I travelled by air from Punjab to Belgium, where I stayed for about a month, locked up in a room with other boys from Punjab. During our stay there, we didn't do much all month, as we couldn't leave the room. I don't know how many other Punjabi boys were with me – maybe, 20 or 25.'

Every day, a few of the men would be allowed to leave the room to undertake the next leg of the journey to England. New migrants arrived from Punjab to take their place. Finally, the day came when it was Kamaljeet's turn to leave. He was instructed to be ready for departure. Within a few hours, he had been packed into a lorry heading for England.

The journey was fraught with risks and not everyone who travelled with him made it to their destination alive. Kamaljeet was well aware of the horror stories associated with illegal migration. He was aware of men suffocating to death during such lorry journeys in the past. He had heard of illegal immigrants killed in knife fights with the smugglers who were transporting them. And he knew of a man from his own hometown in India who had frozen to death while trekking during a leg of the long journey to continental Europe via Russia. But Kamaljeet wasn't deterred by the dangers he was exposing himself to by choosing to undertake the journey.

'I wasn't afraid of the journey. I had wanted this,' he says with a widening smile, revealing a glimmer of the initial excitement and intent he had set forth with. The goal of finding riches in England seemed so attainable to him, the prospect of fulfilling his expectations so real and well worth the risk.

Kamaljeet arrived in England that night in the lorry he had boarded in Belgium and was dropped off in the dark at an unknown location by the motorway. Not knowing where he was, he walked to the closest junction and called a cousin who lived in England to come pick him up.

'There was no one to check my papers. I didn't need to show my passport to anyone that day,' he says.

In the early days following his arrival, he was pleased that his decision to live in England was paying off. Business was thriving.

'I did a lot of building work when I arrived. I've worked all over England – in Bradford, Ilford, Slough – all over,' he says, counting off the cities on the joints of his forefinger.

Like other migrants in Southall, he was able to find day-labour jobs, mostly in construction.

'I helped build so many houses,' he recalls. 'When a builder had a job, he'd give us a call the night before or sometimes, in the morning. Most of the builders we worked with were our people – Indians. I used to work at least six days a week and sometimes, all seven days.'

His words and tone betray a yet unappeased hunger for finding jobs.

'We'd start at eight in the morning, work the whole day and come home at night to shower, prepare dinner and sleep. I lived with a couple of other men from Jalandhar, my town in Punjab, and we became good friends.'

But times have changed. With the immigration issue at the forefront of every election in the UK (a theme echoed across the US and Europe), the Home Office has led a series of crackdowns to combat illegal immigration in those areas across the country that are most densely populated by immigrants. Illegal migrants are summarily deported and anyone found to employ them face heavy fines. It's been more than a year since the jobs stopped coming in for Kamaljeet. The recession and extra-long winters don't help the construction industry either.

'These days, I wake up at ten, take a bath, watch telly and eat roti. I help some people around me to prepare meals. I don't leave my room; I need to stay in all day to avoid being caught. There's no work. I just watch telly all day and wait for others to come back home.'

After years of living and working illegally in London, Kamaljeet has decided it's time to return to his family in Jalandhar, Punjab.

'I've tried to settle here legally. I've even thought about getting married [to someone with a legal status] to stay on here, but my parents won't have any of it. I talk to them on the phone and they've said, "You'll only get married once in your life and it'll be in Punjab." I don't think I could ever marry an Englishwoman, but maybe a nice British Asian?' he laughs.

During the years he was living in London, Kamaljeet's little sister back at home got married. He was unable to attend the wedding, something he says he may regret for the rest of his life.

'My parents are alone now that my sister has got married. They've asked me to return and I'm ready to go home now,' he declares. 'I've had enough.'

Home Office figures indicate that voluntary removals of immigrants like Kamaljeet to their countries of origin, including India, have been steadily rising in the UK over the last few decades, from 335 in 2005 to 15,537 in 2010, with the numbers dipping marginally to 12,879 in 2011. Even as recently as in 2016[4], India and Pakistan were, region-wise, the countries with the largest share of deportees, accounting for a total of 27 per cent of deportees from the UK.

While these statistics reveal a growing realization among potential migrants that the prospect of success in the UK without the legal right to live and work in the country is dim, and the desperate urge to move abroad, especially to make it to London, may not culminate in the fulfilment of a long-cherished dream, the overwhelming desire to earn in pounds and send money back home will persist as long as opportunities for jobs in India are scarce. One EU report on India-to-Europe migrations states that creating 'opportunities for unskilled workers' in India is key to curbing the exodus from the home country of large numbers of people willing to move illegally across international borders in search of employment and a good life[5]. Social pressure on families which do not have members living in other countries, along with pressure on certain members within a single family who have not made it abroad, is yet another issue that needs to be urgently addressed.

Inevitably, among the new arrivals in the UK, those who fare the worst are the undocumented migrants like Kamaljeet, who have neither the credentials nor the legal grounds to live and work in the country.

For some of the immigrants living and working in Southall with valid documentation to justify their stay in the country, the numbers that keep arriving in the borough illegally seem endless. As for those living in Southall illegally, they are facing the hardest times yet.

The smell of ginger and onions crackling in oil fills the winter air as I step off the train. It is dinnertime in Southall. As tired commuters, famished after a hard day's work, rush home to their evening meals, I head to Glassy Junction across the street from the Park Avenue *gurdwara*. The iconic Asian pub, famously featured in Bollywood films like *Dhan Dhana Dhan Goal*, was known to accept payment in Indian rupees. A new owner has taken over the establishment, reincarnated as the popular vegetarian restaurant chain, Saravana Bhavan, but locals still refer to the building as 'Glassy Junction'.

I'm on my way to meet Randeep Lall, a local community activist, for a mid-week dinner. I had heard of him a few years ago, when the international media first splashed the news that dozens of homeless Indian immigrants had been discovered sleeping on the streets of Southall and under the bridges spanning its canals. Illegal immigrants, who had consented to be smuggled into the country with the hope of finding employment opportunities in London, had, in fact, ended up in more dire financial straits than they had been in back in their villages. Randeep was one of the first to assist these migrants and take their stories to the media.

Where the United Sikhs and their Help Desk assist men and women in Kamaljeet's situation with legal advice and make arrangements for them to return to India, Randeep is on the frontlines to help migrants in Southall who are living in poverty and have, inevitably, slipped into drug abuse and homelessness.

A British Sikh, Randeep was born near Southall in the early 1970s and has lived most of his life in neighbouring towns. Having been connected for years to the Asian community in Southall, he's seen it all. He is also one of the first to document the desperate condition of local illegal migrants.

'I've heard it all,' he says, when I meet him.

He tells me about the man who fled a murder charge in India and can never return home. There's another who sold everything he owned to arrange a passport and visa so that he could make his way to England. As for the university-educated Indians who had come all the way here to make their fortunes, they now subsisted on the meagre income they earned from odd jobs – the only kind of work they can get.

'If I had grown up in Southall, I would have become a very different man,' Randeep concedes.

Dressed in a sporty white tracksuit with a black turban on his head, he politely asks me if he can eat while we talk.

Between bites, Randeep outlines for me a rapid social history of the area, highlighting the major tensions of the last few decades that were triggered in the 1950s by the first significant influx of Asians in Southall. The newly arrived immigrants were initially recruited here as factory workers. As they settled down, the ethnic Indian population grew rapidly. In the 1960s, '70s and '80s, residents were witness to simmering tensions as supporters of the far-right National Front found common cause with the neo-Nazi 'skinheads' in targeting the new Asian community. Racial unrest escalated as white parents complained of the changing demographics in local schools and culminated in violence when a Sikh teenager was killed in the '70s. Local Asian gangs like the Holy Smokes and the Tooti Nungs emerged to challenge racial attacks and violence against the community.

The tensions didn't abate with the 'white' population moving out of the area into other neighbourhoods. Asians had to contend with social tensions of their own. The 1990s saw the emergence of gangs like Sher-e-Punjab and Hizb-ul-Tahrir, as conflicts between local Sikhs and Muslims turned to violence. But nothing, apparently, could stem the tide of Asians moving into Southall; unfavourable global circumstances, like civil conflicts in India and Pakistan and the expulsion of Indian settlers from Uganda, forced Asians around the world to find a new home in the UK.

While racial tensions had defined the last few decades, the most crucial issue the area is facing today, according to Randeep, is the constant flow of illegal immigrants arriving at Southall's doorstep.

The local *gurdwara*s provide a frontline of assistance to those who need the bare essentials, as *gurdwara* etiquette mandates that a meal be served to anyone – Sikh or non-Sikh – who enters the temple. Southall has at least ten *gurdwara*s, with each serving an estimated 4,000 meals a day[6]. But as the pleas for help from the growing number of new arrivals in the initial years of the period beginning from 2010 began to become a burden, the *gurdwara*s were unable to handle the influx on their own and reached out to charities and the government for more assistance.

In the course of our meal, Randeep pulls out his mobile and swipes through photo after photo, video after video, sharing with me the enormity of the number of homeless cases he has witnessed in Southall. He, along with his brother, have established an organization called the Sikh Welfare Awareness Team (SWAT) to help these lost, homeless immigrants and relieve the local *gurdwara*s of some of their burden. Every week, you'll find Randeep's SWAT van parked outside the Havelock *gurdwara* in Southall, providing essentials like food, drinking water, clothes and footwear to virtually anyone who appeals for help. He makes it clear that SWAT isn't limited to extending help to Asians alone. On other nights of the week, the van circles around London and has designated spots across the city to provide free hot meals to anyone in need. Randeep remains committed, however, to the existing cases in Southall and the new arrivals who continue to show up here.

'I've seen it with my own eyes,' he tells me. 'Coaches full of students from India arrive in Southall, only for them to realize there aren't any "colleges" here for them to attend.'

Conned by dubious agents in India and with little money to live off, these students have nowhere else to go.

'So they come to the *gurdwara*s for shelter,' Randeep adds.

According to him, word is, somehow, failing to get back to India that if you want to move abroad and London is your targeted destination, you need legal paperwork, enough money to sustain yourself and the will to work hard. The city's streets aren't paved with gold, he remarks wryly.

But the prospect of moving to the UK, even illegally, is still an enticing one for many in India. For all the cases of homelessness and exploitation, there are, of course, thousands of success stories involving Indian immigrants who have not only made it, but made it big in London. In fact, Southall's very own success story is evident in the case of Southall Travel. The little family-owned travel agency which started off by selling flights 'mainly to people we knew', as the owner puts it, is now worth over hundreds of millions, according to *Travel Weekly*[7]. The dream of making millions in London is apparently far more powerful and persuasive than the reality of enduring struggles early in life in a new country. There are even Indians entering the country legally as university students and willing to incur massive debts simply for a chance to acquire the cachet they believe comes from studying overseas.

The reality of life as an illegal immigrant is a far cry from the promises made by agents to people back in India who are open to persuasion and willing to travel to the UK without valid papers. Kamaljeet was eventually deported to India. But he is among the lucky ones. Video testimonials recorded by Randeep give a far more accurate representation of the struggles an illegal migrant must go through simply to survive in Southall.

There's the 50-year-old man who weeps as he describes his predicament in Punjabi: 'In India, we imagine England as a country of endless wealth. I thought I would come here, work hard, make enough money to send back home so that my children and my entire family would be taken care of. But

I've found nothing here. It cost me over 8 lakhs [₹800,000 or nearly £10,000] to travel here. If it wasn't for the assistance I've received from the *gurdwara*, I would be dead by now and no one would ever know.'

Then there is 25-year-old Baljeet from Punjab, who confesses: 'I've been here four years now. The first two years, I worked hard. I did well. But over the last two, I've been trapped in drugs. There are a lot of other brothers like me who are into drugs, mostly heroin. Like me, they also sleep out on the streets in the freezing cold, wherever they can find a space. If we don't take drugs, we can't fall asleep at night. It's just too cold. Without legal papers, not a single person will hire us, and if they do give us work, they won't pay us once the job is done. How can we go back to our families? Now that we're on drugs, we haven't been able to send back any money. How can we go back home and face everyone in this state?'

Randeep had filmed these video testimonials, along with other videos, in his car, using his Blackberry. He hands me his Blackberry now and plays a video interview he had recorded just a few weeks ago; his subject is a homeless man he had found huddled under a bridge nearby in the middle of the night.

As I watch the video, featuring an elderly man with a long silver beard and a loose blue turban, I can't help noticing his bewildered eyes as he asks in Punjabi, 'What next? Where will I go next?'[8]

Notes

1. Axel, Brian Keith (ed.), *From the Margins: Historical Anthropology and its Futures*, Duke University Press Books, 2002.

2. Shields, Niamh, 'London's top five curry houses', *The Guardian*, 27 July 2012.

3. Blinder, Scott, 'Deportations, Removals and Voluntary Departures from the UK', The Migration Observatory, University of Oxford, 4 October 2018.

4. IANS, 'Deportation targets for Indians, Pakistanis reason for UK home minister's resignation?', *Times of India*, 30 April 2018.

5. Saha, K.C., *Irregular Migration from India to the EU: Punjab and Haryana case study*, CARIM – India Project, 2012. .

6. Steel, Mark, 'David Cameron's Christmas raid on Southall's illegal immigrants', *Independent*, 26 December 2013.

7. 'Profile: How Southall Travel broke into the big league', *Travel Weekly*, 3 June 2011.

8. Since the interviews were conducted for this chapter, the number of cases involving homeless Indians living in Southall has been on the decline. Randeep still runs the SWAT organization which has expanded its network of service to the needy around the United Kingdom. The United Sikhs still operate the Help Desk. Neelu and Harbans were honoured with the prestigious British Empire Medal for service in recognition of their work with illegal immigrants.

Cremona, Italy

THE FARMER'S STORY

Thousands of miles from Onkar's home in Cremona, Italy, stands another house in another country. Built with the savings set aside from years of hard work in Italy, Onkar's dream house back in his native Punjab isn't a mere structure with unfurnished spaces and bare walls. Bespoke furniture, carefully covered to protect it from dust, is still waiting to be aired, its showroom newness broken in and comfortably moulded to the shapes of its owners. Steel dishes are meticulously stacked in the kitchen, unused. Duvets and bedspreads, folded into neat squares, sit cold on cupboard shelves. All that is missing from the house is Onkar and his family.

His dream mansion isn't the only house in Punjab that sits unoccupied. In Hoshiarpur district alone, where Onkar's home was built, many houses stand eerily silent, staring out at dusty streets with vacant eyes. The state has enriched itself at the cost of losing its sons and daughters to foreign lands.

Though Onkar has accomplished his dream of building a luxury house in Hoshiarpur, it is a struggle for him to disengage from his life in Italy and return to live in the town where he was born. Will his children, who were raised in Italy, follow him?

A large framed photo of the white marble-fronted house in India hangs in the foyer of Onkar's home in Cremona. He often stops to gaze at the photo, a constant reminder of his dual identity and of the fact that one day, he may need to decide, yet again, which place he should call home. When some leave it all behind and search for adventure abroad, life has a way of coming full circle.

❧

'A lot of the "undocumented" came via Moscow,' Onkar explains to me.

Forty years ago, visas to Russia and its neighbouring countries were easier for Indian nationals to acquire.

'They came with the help of "donkeys" or smugglers,' he continues. 'They mostly flew from India to Moscow and then made their way to Italy. Some took buses, some drove, some walked and some died along the way.' His tone is matter-of-fact.

Onkar himself had arrived in Italy in the 1980s through the proper channels. Over the last few decades, he has worked his way across the country to make a living for his family. Unlike the situation today, with visa restrictions making it difficult for Indians to move to Europe legally without jobs, funding or official sponsorship, it was easier in the '80s to acquire visas and residence permits.

'My first job here was with the circus,' Onkar says, sitting across me at his home in Cremona.

Slurping on a steaming shot of espresso, he enumerates the other odd jobs he has held during his early years in Italy. He looks relaxed in a white Kappa tracksuit, a matching soft turban wrapped around his hair. Then he begins to tell me about the time when he first arrived in Italy.

Onkar had just made the move to Italy from Punjab, India, when he was hired as a driver by the Circo Cesare Togni, one of the country's most popular circus shows in those days. He wasn't the only non-Italian working on the production. Like Onkar, many of the first Punjabi Indians to settle in Italy worked in the amusement-park industry, undertaking demanding jobs like grooming animals and preparing the circus ring[1].

At the time Onkar was hired, the circus was travelling across southern Italy and he was living temporarily in Salerno near the Amalfi Coast. It was a grand enough show to offer work opportunities to a dozen other Punjabi boys who had also recently moved to the country. Tasks – collecting tickets, ushering in spectators and handling the animals, especially the horses – were divided among the group.

In those initial years in the country, a younger Onkar, tall, lean and clad in bell-bottom trousers and patterned shirts, was a driver for the circus, along with two other men. His photos from his youth remind me of my dad's photos from his early days in America – the same style, the same flamboyant posture, the same hearty expression that typified young Punjabi men of those times.

Every night, Onkar would wait as the trapeze artistes inside the tent flew over the audience, accepting the dare to win over the crowds with their aerial acrobatics, and the animal trainers coaxed the performing animals to go through their routine acts.

'The circus performances would go on until midnight,' Onkar recalls.

That was when his own shift began. Circus crews would dismantle the set-up, pack up everything and load the trucks. Onkar drove one of the trucks to the nearest station, where the cargo would get hitched to a freight train and be hauled to the next city. Driving through the night to the same destination, Onkar would wait for the cargo to arrive at the station and move on to the next circus location.

It was good money and truck driving was a fun job for a young man eager to explore and discover a new country. Money and adventure were, after all, the key motivations for Onkar when he had left his family home in Hoshiarpur, Punjab, and flown to Italy.

After a few months of driving for the circus, he picked up a string of jobs along the way to make ends meet. Weeks and months away from home turned into years as he travelled the country, following leads for jobs that mostly came through his Punjabi network of relatives who had settled in Italy – an aunt in Reggio Emilia, a cousin in Rome. With the network expanding over the years, the jobs kept coming. Onkar worked on machines in a factory in Palermo, Sicily. He helped build houses in Amelia. He picked tomatoes in the south of the country. He fixed cars in a village near the mountains to the north.

Italians were kind and accepting of Onkar, and he did his best to fit in, he says, learning to speak the language and even taking the difficult decision of cutting his hair short and removing his turban, as did many other Sikhs, including my father, who had moved out of India around the same time.

Onkar's early years in Italy were taken up by demanding work, but photo albums in his living room reveal that it was a time of happiness for him and other members of the growing community. As others like him, with their roots in Punjab, made the journey to Italy, the already established overseas community of Sikhs here came forward with the help and reassurance that a close-knit family would have offered, accepting the new arrivals into their fold.

Onkar did return to India, but only to marry. Later, his wife and two-year-old daughter, Jess, would join him in Italy. While he had picked up the local language through his interactions with Italians during his varied work experiences, his wife learned to speak Italian by chatting in the garden every morning with their neighbour's talkative wife. So close did they become over the daily Italian lessons that the two couples would even travel together to India to vacation in Onkar's family home in Punjab.

The photos in his home feature the neighbours snuggling up with the family under shared duvets on *manja* benches in Punjab and standing tall in Indian sugarcane fields.

Over the years, Onkar would grow his hair back to its original length and start wearing the turban again, thereby reclaiming the identity he was born with, but had set aside temporarily when he first settled in this country. It was in the early 1990s that he, along with his family, eventually moved to Cremona, where he found permanent work as a *bergammo* or dairy farmer. It was there that I would first meet Onkar and his family and learn why, after all these years in Italy, he still dreams about his house back in India.

It was his daughter, Jess, who introduced me to Onkar.

I had first got in touch with her through email back in 2011. The trigger was an intriguing article in the *New York Times* with the heading, 'In the Italian heartland, Indians keep the cheese coming'. As I read the story, my interest quickened at the idea of this new, close-knit community of Punjabi farmers revitalizing a traditional Italian way of life. Here was a group of Punjabi men and women who had recently emigrated from India to Italy and whose daily work involved producing and sustaining global distribution of cheeses like mozzarella and parmesan. Did they even like the taste of the cheese they were producing, I wondered.

As my curiosity led me to delve deeper into the lives of Punjabi farmers in Italy, I found that little had been written about the community so far. There was, however, one profile featured in the *Hindustan Times*; it was about a Punjabi family living in a town called Cremona – Jess's family.

I sent her an email and soon, we were speaking to each other. I learnt that around the same time that my parents were emigrating to America, Jess's father, Onkar, had moved from India to Italy. With this shared history between us, it was easy for us to establish a connection. Warm and instantly familiar, as if she were my distant cousin, Jess – whose real name is Jaspinder – and I were able to bond over emails and Skype chats. Soon, she was inviting my husband and me to meet her family in provincial Italy, where nearly 16,000 Indians are employed in agriculture. In the province of Cremona where Jess lives, Indians of Punjabi origin represent the single largest immigrant group – around 20 per cent of the total immigrant population in the province – and dominate the dairy-farming industry in Italy today.

Outside the Milano Centrale station, Indian street vendors stand in the driving rain, inadequately protected by papery blue ponchos, and lean in towards us. 'Umbrella? Umbrella?' they repeat in English, smiling as we walk past, their thick Indian accents ringing with their rolling 'R's.

'No, thank you,' we say, smiling back, and head into the station. They turn away and resume their conversations in Punjabi.

Italy is home to around 1,40,000 immigrants from India who come mainly from the northern state of Punjab or the southern state of Kerala. Nearly 80 per cent are from Punjab and have arrived to fill vacancies created by locals, mostly in agriculture. Roman Catholic nurses and nuns from Kerala make up the second-largest group from India, a likely migration, considering Rome's Christian base.

Like Onkar, most Indians living in Italy today arrived here with valid documentation, but an estimated 30 per cent of the Indian population in the country consists of undocumented workers who entered illegally[2]. In the years following India's independence and especially, in recent decades, emigration has burgeoned, but the new hopefuls fall, predominantly, into two categories: low-skilled migrants, who primarily move to the oil-rich Gulf states, like the United Arab Emirates or Saudi Arabia, where they work as labourers; and highly skilled migrants who tend to set their sights on the US, Canada, Australia and the UK. But recent reports of illegal migration from Delhi International Airport reveal that Italy has become the second most-sought-after European destination after the UK, surpassing in demand other countries like Germany and France which, historically, have a more time-honoured tradition of accepting immigrants from other shores.

Many of those who come to Italy illegally have paid

astronomical fees back in India to arrange for their transportation into continental Europe. Some have invested their families' entire savings, accumulated over a lifetime, in this venture. Others sold their homes to finance their journey. A few incurred deep debts to make the journey, lured by the promise of a better future.

Migration routes from India for the purpose of entering Italy illegally are long, arduous and, often, dangerous. A common route for prospective immigrants without bona fide travel documents requires them to take a flight from India to Georgia, a country from which a year-long multiple-entry visa is relatively easy to obtain. The outbound route from Georgia crosses into Turkey and, beyond the latter's borders, into Greece, from where it finally leads to Italy. Another common route involves travel by air to Russia, usually through Moscow, with a bona fide visa and then a switchover to surface transport that takes illegal immigrants to Italy via Ukraine, Slovakia or Hungary. A third, slightly more dangerous option involves travel via sub-Saharan Africa to Morocco, followed by a boat journey to Spain[3].

The message seems clear: thousands of Indians will risk it all to travel abroad in search of job opportunities, social mobility and the prospect of a more fruitful life as an NRI in a foreign country.

Traditionally, Italy was always an 'emigrant-exporting' country. For years, the government focused on strengthening its ties with the Italian diaspora abroad, particularly, in cities like New York and Philadelphia, where many Italians have settled for generations. However, in the last four decades, an expanding economy and an absence of stringent laws to curb migration have transformed Italy into an 'immigrant-receiving' nation facing a mass influx of immigrants from the 1980s onwards. The largest immigrant communities in Italy include Romanians, followed by Albanians, Moroccans, Chinese, Ukrainians and Filipinos. Mass Indian immigration to Italy is a more recent phenomenon, but a rapidly growing one, with an increase of more than 14 per cent between 2010 and 2011. Italy now accounts for the largest Indian population in continental Europe and the second-largest in Europe as a whole, after the UK.

Chain migration or emigration with the help of established networks in the country is a common and recurring pattern among Indians who traditionally rely heavily on village, kin and caste connections and support to make their migration experience a smooth one. In recent years, people like Onkar, who arrived in the country in the '80s and were able to secure work and build a home, have made Italy a viable destination for many fellow Indians back home, who are keen to do the same. Those who settled in Italy have been calling their parents, siblings, cousins and friends over from India and encouraging them to join them in their adopted country on a long-term basis.

Though Italy has gone through a recession in recent years, the earlier large-scale economy of its northern and central regions may have served as a significant financial incentive for immigrants to move to the country. As remittances to India from

Italy increased, so did the attraction of moving to this country. In fact, Tuscany is now home to the second-highest number of Indians living in the country. But the largest concentration of Indians in Italy is to be found in the northern region of Lombardy, particularly, in the province of Cremona.

For hundreds of Punjabi families living in Italy, including Onkar's, all roads lead to Cremona. And that is where I will also head.

The direct train from Milan to Cremona takes hardly an hour to reach its destination. On this grey, overcast day, the outskirts of Milan look like a depressing canvas of construction and graffiti. The incomplete structures of cold concrete buildings, hollow and still uninhabitable, match the steel-grey rainclouds above. Other buildings that were once inhabited have been reduced to rubble, presumably to make way for new constructions.

As the train halts at towns like Lodi and Codogna along the way, I read station signs like '*sottopassagio* (subway)' and try to imagine how alien this language would seem to someone who has just arrived from rural India.

It's not long before Milan is behind us. As our train moves on, derelict blocks recede into the distance and suburban scenes appear, giving way to rural landscapes that pass swiftly by our compartment window. Puddles of rainwater sparkle in the fields of earthy reds and green and, in the distance, silos and brick farmhouses stand as they have for decades. In this flat landscape that unfolds like Punjab's vast farming lands, iconic red-tiled roofs crown brick homes and remind us that we are in Italy.

Sixty miles beyond the outskirts of Milan, the province of Cremona, with a capital city that bears the same name, lies to the north of the Po River valley. Our hotel is located just outside the town centre. The capital is best known for its musical traditions and instruments, particularly, the violins that were made there between the sixteenth and eighteenth centuries, and the two museums near the town centre, showcasing the meticulous handcrafting of this instrument.

Apart from its rich history of music, the province is a vital agrarian centre in Italy's dairy and agricultural heartland. The food industry is a leading economy in Cremona, with chocolate factories and cheese makers populating its countryside. A map of nearby towns reads like a menu of familiar Italian cheeses or *formaggio*: towns like Parmigiano-Reggiano and Grana Padano produce cheeses of the same name, originally made by monks, and Ricotta and Gorgonzola are also made locally. These local *formaggio* are some of Italy's most popular cheeses and exports.

But as in the case of the dying art of handcrafting violins, there has been a dramatic decline in interest among the country's younger generation of workers with regard to preserving traditional Italian techniques of dairy production for cheese. In the late 1980s, the shortage of farmers became so severe, in fact, that many of the dairy farms which had been traditionally passed down within families from one generation to the next were shut down and abandoned. Realizing that an entire Italian way of life was nearing extinction, the government began considering remedial measures. Before long, the Italian countryside had become home to thousands of farmers from Punjab, India's agricultural heartland.

Among the foreign nationals who work in the agricultural sector in Italy, Indians are the second-most numerous group after the Albanians. Like Onkar, in the north, most Punjabi Indians work as cow milkers, known as *bergamini* in Italian. About 90 per cent of the workers in the dairy industry are Indian. Many of them also serve as ancillary staff, transporting milk and other dairy products to their destinations[4]. In fact, members of Coldiretti, Italy's leading agricultural organization, had declared in 2009 that the emblematic Italian cheese industry would be at risk without the contribution of its Indian workers.

While the inconvenient work hours, with multiple daily shifts, have made the job of dairy farming less appealing to young Italians, working in the *stalle* or cowsheds ensures stability in comparison to other agricultural work which is seasonal and highly unpredictable. The position of a cow milker also offers the advantage of a *contratto indeterminato* or permanent contract, with job security and benefits like paid annual holidays, making this kind of work a very attractive deal for Onkar and others in the community[5]. There is room for exploitation, though. Illegal immigrants – or *clandestini*, as they are locally known – who work in agriculture without any legal contracts to protect their interests often end up being paid as little as three euros an hour, despite being made to work for up to 15 hours a day. The plight of those who had engaged the services of a *caporalato* or job broker to acquire a position is more desperate still; they are forced to hand over to the middleman a cut of their wages and end up with a slave-like take-home pay of 80 cents an hour[6].

Despite such drawbacks, the job of a *bergammo* has been perceived, on the whole, as a highly attractive one by an entire generation of Indians who moved from farms in Punjab to farms in Cremona, where job stability and better financial prospects seemed more assured than back home in rural Punjab. People follow the jobs, and in the 1990s, there were jobs galore for Punjabi farmers in Italy.

A smiling Jess arrives at our Cremona hotel and embraces us warmly as we meet in person for the first time. Over the next few days, she will introduce me to her community and her family, and welcome us into her home.

A petite 23-year-old, Jess majored in languages at the University of Verona. She switches effortlessly from Italian to English and then to Punjabi, the language she learnt first as a child in India. Born in Hoshiarpur, Punjab, she had moved to Italy when she was two years old to join her father, Onkar.

'This is not a strange country to me,' Jess says. 'For me, Italy is home.'

Her family wasn't alone in moving to Italy. Many of the people in the Italian–Punjabi community can trace their journey back to a home in Hoshiarpur.

'We're like a mini Hoshiarpur here,' Jess laughs, as she drives us down country lanes early on a Sunday morning, joking about the road-hogging tendencies of drivers in Italy as a motorist cuts her off. 'All our family is here now. We have no one left in Punjab.'

Italy is where Jess feels at home, but she maintains close ties with her Punjabi culture and Sikh faith. She regularly visits the nearby *gurdwara* in Cremona which serves as a community centre for the growing local Sikh population. As a first-generation Sikh Italian, she, along with others like her at the *gurdwara*, faces issues that first-generation Indian immigrants confront around the world, having to explain their culture to the local population. At the *gurdwara*, Jess and her friends have published literature written in Italian to explain the fundamental principles of the Sikh faith to the local community in an effort to ease racial tensions. A book they've brought out called *La corona di stoffa* ('the crown of tissue') explains the geography and history of Sikhs in India. The book that includes chapters entitled '*La storia del turbante*' and '*Prima e seconda guerra mondiale e i Sikh*' provides the necessary context for understanding why Sikhs wear turbans and how they fought during both World Wars. Approximately 50,000 Indians, then British subjects and soldiers in the British Imperial Army, had fought on Italian soil during World War II as part of the 8th Army; 5,782 of those soldiers had lost their lives in Italy[7].

'It's important to study your roots just to be able to explain to your future generation who you are,' says Jess. 'Because obviously, I could be an Italian citizen, but my skin colour is not white. So I'll always have to answer that one question from people: "Where do you come from?"'

In Cremona, winters are foggy and summers sticky, thanks to the river that cuts through the province. This morning is wet and cold, typical of January, and we are offered piping hot tea in steel glasses the moment we enter the *gurdwara* where we've spent the first part of the day with Jess. The kitchen is buzzing with activity as *sevadars* or volunteers prepare the meals that will be served to all who visit the *gurdwara*. It is a Sunday and hundreds of local members are expected to attend the service.

The stairs leading to the main prayer hall are outside, hugging the temple's exterior walls. At the top of the stairs is a landing, somewhat like a spacious balcony, inviting the outdoors in, as it were. From here, the view is unhindered; stretching for miles is green agricultural land on which work many of the families present at the *gurdwara* today. Visible, too, are dairy houses which employ several of the others gathered here.

I take a seat inside and listen to the hymns sung by visiting Sikhs from Austria. Everything about the *gurdwara* and the people within it seems familiar: the rural Punjabi dialect, the sounds of Indian musical instruments being played, the silks and sequins adorning the women, along with their favourite accessory, deep maroon lipstick, the buttery scented aromas rising from the kitchen – an entire lifestyle inspired by a culture originating thousands of miles away, all housed in a structure designed by an Italian architect.

As the services come to a close, there are a few community-related announcements. A local member has suffered a heart attack. Could we please collect donations for his family? Also, a cultural programme will be held in Milan next week; the youth are encouraged to attend.

I mingle with some of Jess's friends at the *gurdwara*. Jaswant Singh, who moved to Italy from Punjab years ago, is one of them. He now leads the Sunday school at the *gurdwara* and speaks passionately about language. His eyes linger on his daughter as he talks about the 'treasure of our mother tongue' and the need to teach the next generation of Italian Indians how to read, write and speak Punjabi. But equally important, he says, is the need to teach newly arrived immigrants the Italian language.

'I still have days where my head hurts from speaking in Italian, but thinking in Punjabi,' he confesses.

Sitting quietly in the corner of the room in a powdery pink salwar kameez is Jaswant's wife, who recently joined him from Punjab and is still settling in. Her gaze rests on their daughter, a bubbly three-year-old who responds when addressed in either Punjabi or Italian. Jaswant's wife was educated in India and finished university there, but without a working knowledge of spoken Italian, she feels barely literate and completely at sea.

'It's not like we keep our wives locked up at home,' Jaswant explains. 'It just takes [them] some time to learn the language before they can start working and feeling at ease in the Italian community.'

Like many of the other men at the *gurdwara*, Jaswant works at a local factory as an inventory manager. Others that I speak to work in chocolate factories, cheese-making houses or dairy farms like Jess's father and uncle.

We stand in the rain-soaked fields under wide-canopied umbrellas, the kind with a loop to hold onto at the end. It is drizzling and cold enough to see our breath vaporize. I wish I were indoors, sitting with Jess by the wood stove.

On our way to her home, we visit her cousins and her uncle, who also works in a dairy farm. Paolo, one of the cousins, is giving us a tour of the lands and the farm where his father works and where the farmhouse he lives in stands. Paolo points to the acres of fields that stretch away into the distance. In the summer, those fields will be full of tall maize and wheat.

'You should come back to visit in summer to see how everything is growing in the fields,' he suggests.

Paolo speaks faltering English and we communicate mostly in polite, broken Punjabi. He is most comfortable speaking Italian and with his sandy brown eyes and Italian fashion sense – skinny black jeans and a cream wool jumper – he could easily pass for an 'Italiano'.

If I didn't know his real name was Gurpal – 'Please, call me Paolo,' he urges – I would never have guessed that he was of Indian heritage. Just as Jaspinder has become Jess, Gurpal has become Paolo. He explains that many Indians in Italy have two names: a traditional Indian one and an Italian one for locals to pronounce easily in school or at the workplace. Most of Paolo's friends at university are Italian and he feels accepted by his country, Italy, he says.

'This is my country,' he declares.

'You must be popular with the ladies at your university,' I tease him.

He gives me a sheepish smile and carries on walking down the muddy path.

During his recent visits to India, he found it too hot and dirty to live in permanently. He is far happier in Italy with his friends, his job and his home. Besides, he prefers football to cricket. I can't imagine Paolo agreeing to relocate to India if his parents ever decided to move back. After meeting his father, I realize that such a decision would, in all likelihood, never be forced on the young man.

We follow Paolo carefully down the path, flanked by rain-moist fields on either side. I tread cautiously so that my feet don't sink into the deep puddles we must step over as we move along the path. As we approach the farm, we see cows – dozens of them – boxed into a holding area where the bulky animals spend their days chewing the cud in a leisurely fashion as the hours pass by.

Paolo leads us inside the farm to the place where his father and two other men from Punjab milk the cows every day.

'Come, let me introduce you to my father,' he offers.

Paolo's father, Hardeep Singh, comes up a flight of stairs from the milking area below to greet us. He apologizes for not being able to shake hands. 'Mine are filthy,' he explains softly, nervously clasping his rubber-gloved hands together.

Hardeep is in his mid-fifties. The lower part of his face is covered in white stubble and, though a brown wool hat keeps his head warm, his nose has reddened from being out for hours in the cold. His eyes are gentle and there is something about his low-browed forehead that suggests humility.

Hardeep had arrived in Italy in the late '70s and began work as a *bergammo* years later. He's been with this particular *stalle* for nearly ten years and looks after around 270 cows, he informs us. The hours of work are spread over an entire day, starting at 2 a.m. and finishing at 6 a.m., with the next shift resuming at 2 p.m. and continuing until 6 p.m.

'Milk must be absolutely fresh to produce *formaggio*,' Hardeep explains in Punjabi, though I note that he has pronounced '*formaggio*' the Italian way. 'To ensure that the milk is as fresh as it can be, drivers from the cheese factories collect it from us twice a day – at seven in the morning and then at seven in the evening.'

Local Indians work as cheese producers as well as milk farmers; and often, the drivers who are sent to collect the milk and the employees of the dairy farms are friends. As far as the cheese producers are concerned, their shift begins with the collection of the milk which they then incorporate into their own ongoing production cycle that lasts through the night and into the following day.

'The money is good and Italian bosses are generally kind and reliable,' Hardeep says of dairy farming as a profession. 'At least, mine have been. There are, of course, bosses who cheat you out of hard-earned money, but my bosses have always been kind and have paid me my just dues.'

With the recession hitting Italy, however, the last few years have been tough. Farms have shut down and work is harder to find for the newer arrivals from Punjab. If the problem of *nasha* or drugs weren't so acute in Punjab and job opportunities were more plentiful there, Hardeep says he would encourage youngsters to stay home and work hard, instead of moving to Italy.

'I've been here for so many years now,' he replies with some reluctance, when I ask him if he would ever consider moving back to Punjab. 'I have bought a house here, raised my children here. The children have studied and have their own jobs now. I even have an Italian passport. I'm settled.

'Almost all of my family has moved out of Punjab. Most of them are here in Italy now, except my parents. My mother and father were still in Punjab and...'

He stops in mid-sentence. He looks at me in helpless silence and his face crumples. Unable to release his pent-up feelings, Hardeep simply shakes his head. Tears stream down his face.

'It's okay,' Paolo quietly intervenes. 'His father passed away three years ago and he still cries when he thinks about him.'

'I'm all right.' Speaking through his tears, Hardeep smiles apologetically.

Initially, I am nervous about speaking to Onkar. His thick greyish beard camouflages his smile and, with the broad shoulders of a National Football League player, he cuts a rather intimidating figure.

Onkar routinely sets out for his workplace just before midnight. In those quiet hours, he slips into his work clothes, wraps his turban around his head, then sips a quick espresso by the kitchen table before leaving home, with his wife and two children still fast asleep upstairs. He drives down an unlit country road to the *stalle* where he's worked for the past ten years. The shift runs from midnight to around six in the morning; then it starts again from two in the afternoon to around eight in the evening. Onkar works seven days a week.

Working in the cowshed alongside another Punjabi workers and the farm's Italian owner, he manages milk production and oversees the health of around 160 cows. The milk produced at the farm where he works is used locally to produce cheeses like Grana Padano.

When we first meet him at the dairy farm, Onkar is busy wiping the machines that milk dozens of cows simultaneously. The bovines look down at me, wide-eyed and uncertain, and

I stand behind Onkar, astonished by the quantity of cow milk that humans are capable of consuming. Onkar hardly utters a word as he moves rapidly from one task to the next, carrying out the manual chores that have defined the muscles in his body and the pattern of his life in Italy.

As he moves from one cow to the next, I duck and jump aside to avoid being splattered by the steaming hot dung being released all around us.

'If you don't mind, I'll speak to you at home,' he finally says to me in Punjabi, softly adding, 'you're scaring the cows.'

Before I can make my way out of the pit where Onkar and his machines milk the cows standing above them, he murmurs a few words in Italian. As if on command, the cows begin moving forward, rotating through the queue, making room for the next set of bovines to be milked. As these multi-tonne creatures circle freely around me, I'm convinced that if anyone is scared, it's me. Onkar, however, knows the creatures well, and they obey him as he gently directs their movements, speaking to them all the while in Italian.

For the second night in a row, we go to Jess's home for dinner. Onkar and his wife, Balvir, insist that we have our meals at their home; they seemed genuinely disappointed that we've chosen to stay at a hotel, even though this is the first time we're meeting.

Their home is beautiful and inviting. In summer, they sit downstairs where the marble floors keep the space cool. Upstairs, with its open-face fireplace and heavy silk curtains, is for the winter months. I spend most of my time sitting in the country-style kitchen, a long, airy space, meticulously clean and clutter-free, but for the collection of figurines that stand above the stove – the three wise men, along with Yoda and Shrek, standing side by side. Balvir, a warm, jolly woman, laughs loudly as she stares at the figurines and admits that she can't remember why they are there.

'The kids, I'm sure,' she says.

A TV sitting atop the fridge beams out Indian satellite channels. Right now, the Sikh channel is on and evening prayers blare loudly from the screen as our hostess rolls the dough for dinner. Jess and her brother, Gurminder, whose local name is Giulio, search the kitchen for the remote to change the channel. Their mother asks about my parents and my in-laws, and insists they should all come and visit Cremona. She chats with me as if I were family and not a complete stranger she is meeting for the first time.

When Onkar comes home, he places in the fridge a bottle of fresh milk from the farm – a daily ritual. The fresh milk makes the tea thick and creamy, a meal in itself, and Balvir also makes Indian paneer for dinner from this milk.

Unlike in London, where 'curry' and 'tikka' dishes are staples of the national diet and Indian restaurants proliferate, such eateries are few and far between in Italy. As Jess and I chat while dinner is being prepared, I ask her about the kind of food they eat regularly at home; is it Italian or Indian cuisine? My mouth waters just thinking about the options they have.

'In Italy, eating is everything, just like in Punjab,' she explains. 'Italian [cuisine] is the mother of food, but in our house, we mix it up.'

Her mother's favourite meal includes the rich traditional Punjabi dish of *saag* or spinach which used to be made regularly in her kitchen back in India. But the family is addicted to pizza and Sunday night at Jess's house is always pizza night.

'But you'll see our pizzas covered in onions and chillies,' she laughs.

Those are fresh, home-grown chillies, actually. While Jess's father works long hours at the dairy farm, her mother tends to her own little farm at the back of the house.

'She keeps a [vegetable] garden and is obsessed with growing green chillies and coriander,' Jess explains. 'She's made friends with all the neighbours, because she gives away vegetables from her garden to everyone.'

While we're chatting at the kitchen table, Onkar has gone upstairs to change out of his work clothes. Yesterday, when we were here for dinner, he had changed into a comfortable track suit and his hair was wrapped in a small turban. This evening, he comes down dressed smart – brown trousers, a shiny collared shirt with a matching cardigan, dress shoes and a proper turban, pleated and wrapped so that it sits proudly on his head.

'Why are you so dressed up?' we all ask, surprised.

'Come, let me show you around Cremona,' Onkar offers, gesturing to my husband and me.

His innate sense of hospitality is overwhelming, undiminished by the tiring afternoon work shift he has completed or the thought of the next shift that is due to begin in about six hours in the middle of the night.

'Look, Jess is my daughter and you are just like Jess in my eyes,' he says to me in Punjabi, as though I am a surrogate child from the diaspora. 'You are visiting and we are happy to take you out.'

Traditional Indian hospitality, expressed through the old Sanskrit phrase, '*Atithi devo bhava*', implying that guests are to be revered like gods, is alive and well in Onkar's home which is as inviting and warmly welcoming as any in Punjab. Perhaps, more so, because meeting another Punjabi in Cremona is still a bit of a novelty. The swiftness with which we all connect and fall into an easy cultural familiarity is a clear reflection of the power of the diaspora network, which allows us to bond instantly over shared histories, language, food and cultural etiquette.

No, we insist repeatedly in response to Onkar's invitation to take us out, he ought to rest. He finally heeds our words and relaxes, offering to take us on a tour of their back garden instead. We are amazed by what we see there. Tomato vines and bunches of garlic hang from an archway leading into a garden full of vegetables, along with the coriander and chillies so dear to Onkar's wife. A home-made water system irrigates the vegetable patch, sparing Onkar and his wife this extra chore.

At the front of the house, pear, cherry and apricot trees line the garden.

I return to the kitchen. On the table, Balvir has set a plate of fresh mozzarella and tomatoes, alongside the Indian dinner of roti, rice, paneer and vegetable curry.

'Do you like *desi* ghee with your curry?' she asks, holding a steel jar of the clarified butter she has made herself.

I decline. 'It's too fattening.'

'Maybe, for you and me,' she grins. 'But for the men, they work hard all day at the farm. They deserve a little extra butter now and then.' With a smile, she plops a generous blob of the home-made butter into the curry.

Every bite of the meal is deeply satisfying and after dinner, we go upstairs to sit by the open-air fireplace in their lounge. Relaxed, with his feet up, a smiling Onkar shares his story.

Sitting around the fireplace, we crack open peanuts in their shells and toss the shells into the fire. Onkar sips on an espresso, even though he will be going to bed soon.

'Espresso does nothing for me,' he confesses.

He tells us about his first job in Italy with the circus and goes on to describe how he had moved around the country in search of employment. He shows us photos from his early days in Italy. Then he goes back even further.

'Back in India, my family were *kissans* – farmers. We had

land and we always had four or five cows on our land. But over there, we never did this work of looking after the cows. We had *bhaiya*s to do the job. But now, I do the job of a *bhaiya*,' he laughs.

Onkar has lived in Cremona since the mid-1990s, when he finally settled into a steady profession – that of a dairy farmer. For nearly ten years, he worked in one farm, before moving to the one where he's now employed.

'In my last job, I just milked the cows, but now I do everything. I've learned how to take care of the cows and even treat them with medicines [when they are ill]. *Gayanan di kum* (or milking cows) is good work. Any job is good if it pays well.'

Balvir agrees. 'In Italy, they give you a lot for farming. They give you a house and look after you. They don't treat you like labourers, the way they do in India,' she says. 'Back in our home in India, we never treated people like that. People who looked after the animals, [the] *bhaiya*s, they ate with us. We looked after their needs as well. But not everyone does that.'

'Yes, it's good over here,' Onkar adds. 'But when my parents came and saw how hard we worked here, they said, "If you worked this hard in India, you wouldn't have needed to move abroad. You could have made a life there."'

Onkar and Balvir lapse into silence for a moment. I'm not unfamiliar with his parents' point of view. I've heard the same opinion expressed by many people I met.

'But back then, we were young,' Onkar continues, 'we avoided working on the family farm. We just wanted to go abroad.'

Unlike for some who are driven by necessity to make the trip overseas, it was his innate sense of adventure and the compulsion to seek his fortune that had led Onkar to move to Italy.

'Now it does occur to me, sometimes, that had I worked this hard there, we could have had so much in India,' he muses. 'There's so much potential to be explored back home.

'For everyone back in Punjab who wants to come here now, I understand why they want to, but I wouldn't advise it. Things have changed. There's a recession in Italy, it's hard to find work and even some of the farms are closing down. It's a hard life outside [overseas] and it takes so much money to leave India. Here in Italy, some are [even] committing suicide.'

He is referring to cases where people, buckling under the pressure of repaying the money they had spent to emigrate from India to Italy, had ended up killing themselves.

'Three or four years ago, it was happening a lot. Some were consuming poison, while others set themselves on fire. They had incurred major debts to travel all the way from India and when they arrived here, there was no work for them. Their parents wanted them to send money back to pay off the debt. What were they supposed to do? They didn't even have money for food.

'If I could advise them, I would tell them not to come at all. But I understand the reason why people want to go abroad.

Before we go back home [to India] for a visit, we save money so that we have enough to spend a month-long holiday there, to drive around in nice cars, to shop for new clothes. It gives the impression that we have a lot of money. But no one gets to see how hard we have to work here.'

Onkar's mood turns sombre. It's when people go back to India with gifts from Europe, pockets full of cash and fanciful stories about their improved new lives abroad that they fuel misconceptions about the rewards of making a life outside India, he says.

'Sometimes, people [Indians living abroad] make it seem as if the streets are paved with gold in Europe and America, but the truth is that you have to work very hard to make a living anywhere in the world.

'I once went back to India with a few other boys who live here. We all do the same kind of work. We all worked together in the farms. But when they went back, one told everyone that he works in a car factory; the other said he drives big trucks. I made fun of him and said, "You don't drive a truck. If anything, you push a wagon around the farm."'

Stories like these are responsible for creating false expectations and perpetuating get-rich-quick illusions, along with the notion that life abroad as an NRI is easy.

'Look, up until now, I've never lied about what I do,' Onkar says. 'I've never stolen anything. I've always worked honestly to earn my money. There's no big or small work – it's all the same. Work with honesty.'

His convictions and his contentment, apparent in his words, remind me so much of my dad, who has found peace in coming to terms with the way his life has turned out, though it may be quite different from how he had envisaged it in his youth. With Onkar too, working on a dairy farm might not have been the dream he had nurtured when he left India for Italy all those years ago. But he now talks about his work with pride.

'We've built a huge house in India; you can see the photo hanging downstairs,' Onkar tells me. 'It's been about two years since it was completed, but it's sitting there, empty. We can't let that house go, but we can't abandon this one either. We're stuck. We can't go back. The children are studying at university here. So we can't leave them and set off. We have a home here now.' He looks at Gurminder and Jess sitting next to him on the sofa.

Onkar is voicing the sentiments of so many immigrants who had left home with short-term plans to make some money and return to India after a few years, not imagining that they would put down roots in foreign soil and build an entirely new life for themselves abroad.

'I don't know if we will ever move back to India permanently – especially, if the children are settled here,' Onkar muses. 'But at least, we have a place back home to return to. We can always go back.'

'We could always live there for six months and here for six months. Besides, we'll see where she settles,' Balvir says, playfully hinting at Jess to get married soon.

'Why does the conversation always lead back to me getting married?' Jess asks indignantly.

Onkar laughs and continues, 'Sometimes, if I have a bad day at work or if my boss is being rude, I think, "If I worked on my own farm back in India, I wouldn't have to listen to someone telling me off." At the farm where I used to work, the Italian boss was also my landlord, as we lived in his farmhouse. He would always remind me that he was the owner. "This is my land," he would repeat. But I would tell myself, "It's okay, he's right." But now that we've bought our own house, I feel so free. We can drill holes in the wall to hang things as we please. It's our house. We don't need to ask for permission. We can host visitors now. You can stay with us.'

Onkar revels in his achievement of having bought his own house in Cremona, but it's the freedom of living in his custom-built house in his hometown that he sometimes pines for.

'We can't go anywhere,' he says, torn between his dream of living in the house in Punjab and his obligations in Italy. 'I earned money and bought land in Italy. I built a home in India. I did it all by working hard. If the family is happy, I am happy. The children are studying. They are working hard. I am content.'

'My father has achieved so much in life,' Jess says proudly. 'And he's put all his efforts into educating us. I'm working on a postgraduate degree in Economics and my younger brother is at university, studying architecture. I don't think we'll ever work in the dairy farms like my father.'

'I sometimes think I'll work here until I start getting pension, but who can last that long – they keep increasing the age limit for receiving pension,' Onkar says, laughing. 'I do dream that maybe, one day, the time will come when we can go back to India. But right now, it doesn't seem likely. Right now, we can't do a thing – we can't leave our work, our children, our home here.'

It's late and Onkar needs to get some sleep before his midnight shift begins. As we make our way down the stairs and pause near the door, saying our farewells, I look up at the photo of the house in Punjab once again.

Onkar catches my glance. 'It's beautiful, isn't it?' he smiles, his expression both tender and wistful.

Notes

[1] Lum, Kathryn, 'The Quiet Indian Revolution in Italy's Dairy Industry', CARIM-India Research Report 2012/08.

[2] Saha, K.C., *Irregular Migration from India to the EU: Punjab and Haryana case study*, CARIM-India Project, 2012.

[3] Ibid.

[4] Lum, Kathryn, 'The Quiet Indian Revolution in Italy's Dairy Industry', CARIM-India Research Report 2012/08.

[5] Ibid.

[6] Ibid.

[7] Bedi, Harchand Singh, 'The Legendary 8th Army – Italy', Sikhnet. com.

Montreal, Canada

A LIFE IN FRENCH

I often wonder if my prayers sometimes go unanswered because I communicate with God in faltering Punjabi. Is my use of Punjabi grammar totally incomprehensible? Despite such doubts, I resist communicating with him in English, my first language, because my idea of religion and spirituality is a gift that was bestowed on me in a different medium altogether – the language of my parents' earliest home.

During the years my brother and I were growing up, our parents would speak to us in a mix of Punjabi and English. They chose the latter when asking us about school and studies, but fell back on the former when discussing the more intimate details of life – our daily routine, what was for dinner, who was coming over to visit – and more importantly, the values and principles which served as the foundation of our formative years. Punjabi was the language in which I was comforted, inspired and disciplined. It was the language of my inner world, just as English served as the medium for dealing with matters which lay outside it. Regardless of how many decades my parents have lived in America – and so many of their generation do – they still lapse into Hindi and Punjabi while greeting each other and when they wish to speak freely, spontaneously, without having to choose their words with care. The language still connects them to each other and to their past in India, as it does for so many others who move abroad.

An immigrant's first language is 'an essential link to their own personal, religious and cultural origin, to their parents and to other members of their families and as the only bond to an essential part of their lives they had to leave behind,' states one study carried out by the University of Vienna[1] about the language needs of adult immigrants. It goes on to say, '...the first language belongs to the kernel of their identity – it is the language in which they started to realise themselves as persons (personal identity), as members of a family and social group (social identity), and in which they developed values important for their lives (cultural/ religious identity).'

Just as language can be a valuable source of personal identity and unity within a community, it can, equally, act as a stumbling block, a major obstacle that stands in the way of communication, preventing new immigrants from reaching out and navigating a new life and hindering their ability to access necessary services, find employment and interact with the wider community. Language barriers can reduce a well-educated professional into an outsider with poor communication skills or isolate a cosmopolitan, city-bred individual from her wider social environment, forcing her into the unfamiliar role of a housebound loner. Language has the power to both touch the heart and erect walls.

These thoughts are on my mind when I visit Montreal, the largest city in Quebec, a Canadian province where the majority official language is French. While Canada has always attracted Indians in large numbers, I have often wondered how those among them who chose to move to Montreal deal with the language of their adopted state. Thanks to Bill 101, Quebec's 1977 Charter of the French Language, 95 per cent of the population in the province speaks the language. While English and other languages are also spoken and respected, according to the Bill, French is intended to serve in Quebec as 'the language of Government and the Law, as well as the normal and everyday language of work, instruction, communication, commerce and business'.

I had somehow imagined that the need for proficiency in the language would make it a less appealing destination for Indians emigrating abroad, but the reality is that, in recent years, Montreal has become a top draw for Indian students wishing to pursue university-level studies. The reasons are clear: it is easier to obtain a visa for higher studies here, and tuition fees are significantly lower, as is the cost of living, than in other destinations like the US and the UK.

The drive up to Montreal will take us just under five hours.

We are heading to the city over the Valentine's Day weekend which promises to be one of the year's coldest. We have chosen to set out, it seems, on a freezing winter's day in every sense of the term, with the temperature plunging to a low of -25 degrees Celsius.

As we enter the island of Montreal, low clouds hover over the frozen St Lawrence River. Gusts of snowdrift graze across the road ahead of us. From afar, it seems as if we are driving into dense white fog, but as we cut through it, we find ourselves surrounded by funnels of snow that refuse to settle.

We have come prepared with snow boots, fur-trimmed hoodies, thick, fleece-lined gloves and other extreme-weather gear, but they don't seem up to the task of protecting us from the savage bite of Montreal's arctic winter; in the few minutes it takes us to yank our suitcases out of the car boot and hurry to the hotel entrance, the exposed skin on our faces nearly freezes over in the sharp, ice-cold air; the sensation is one of being stung repeatedly. We wonder how, under the circumstances, we will spend the next few days in the city.

We have a packed schedule ahead of us, with plans to explore the heart of Montreal, a lively, cosmopolitan and student-friendly city. We also intend to venture out to its outskirts and head for a neighbourhood called Park Extension, an area where you'll find Indian restaurants, stores and a small Indian population. While Canada is a popular destination for Indians to emigrate to, with cities like Toronto and Vancouver claiming the highest density of Indian population in the country, Montreal, too, has an Indian community scattered in neighbourhoods across the city. I wonder how those Indians who moved to this city cope in a province that is proud of its bilingualism, while keeping up with the native languages they had spoken back in India. It's one thing to pick up a new language in a new country, but another to learn and communicate effectively in two languages – English and French. It must feel strange and a little disconcerting, as if you're adding an extra layer between your life as a Canadian and your life back home in India.

We spend the next day moving around the city, insulated from head to toe in warm winter gear. We could have spared ourselves the bitter cold by exploring Montreal's 'underground city', an area full of shops and restaurants under the city's downtown area, but we choose, instead, to stay outdoors. We visit Vieux-Montréal or Old Montreal, walking along the famed 'cobblestone' streets in the area that every travel guide highlights so effusively. On this cloudy, wintery day, Vieux-Montréal truly resembles Europe's most charming streets and, for a moment, it is possible to forget that you are in Canada.

Later, as we're driving up to the top of Mont Royal, the mini-mountain or hill that is the city's namesake, I see many covering the same route on foot. It is beyond me how others are able to trek up to the summit in the bitter cold, and I am grateful that I don't have to do the same. On reaching the top, I am content to simply walk around for a few minutes, long enough to manage a selfie and take in the panoramic view of the city, beautiful under a mantle of snow.

That night, we have a Valentine's Day dinner date downtown at Le Taj. Over our meal of classic Indian dishes, we meet the owner who tells us that he has been a resident of Montreal for several decades and that his restaurant now attracts visiting Bollywood celebrities and American politicians. The Indian waiters whom we chat with confide that life is good in Montreal, but for the bother of having to learn to communicate in French.

Emboldened by our luck at having sailed through our first day in Montreal, unscathed – we've managed to avoid frostbite – we're already looking forward to our next day there and hold high hopes that our plan to venture past the city centre will yield interesting sights and experiences.

Park Extension is less than a 30-minute drive from our hotel, with McGill University and Mont Royal lying en route. The area we're heading for lies in Montreal's borough of Villeray–Saint-Michel-Parc-Extension at the north end of Park Avenue and is literally an 'extension' of the centre. Hence the name.

Traditionally an 'immigrant corridor', with a history of accommodating Jewish, Italian and Greek immigrant communities, Park Extension today is home to immigrants who have arrived mostly from South Asia, India, Bangladesh and Pakistan.

We park near Rue Jean-Talon to grab a bite before the

interview I have lined up at the local Park Extension community library, where students whose mother tongue is not French can learn to speak the language.

Along the way, we pop into one of the local stores which offer a random mix of low-priced goods. It's one of those places where you can find dustpans and lipsticks in the same aisle for the same price. It is here that I meet Mohamad.

A tall, skinny young man with jet-black hair and an easy smile, he stands behind the till, rustling through some papers and pausing every few minutes to check his buzzing mobile. He looks bored and I sense that he is happy to chat with me as I self-consciously browse through the random products arranged on the shelves, hardly sparing a look at them. My intention is not to buy, but to engage the young man in conversation.

Mohamad is studying part-time at the local Concordia University, majoring in Electrical Engineering. When he's not attending classes, he works here at the store. He tells me that he's originally from Andhra Pradesh and came to Montreal last August to study. Speaking in slow, careful English, he shares his experience of navigating the language barriers in the province.

'I've had to learn basic French, so I can at least understand what everyone is saying,' he confides.

Unlike in some of the other universities in the area which are francophone, the medium of instruction at Concordia is English, but around the city and in the province of Quebec, it's useful to have a working knowledge of French. Besides this language, of which he is picking up more and more everyday, Mohamad also speaks Urdu, Telugu, Hindi and, of course, English.

Despite the linguistic challenges that Montreal presents, the young man chose to study here. The reason, he explains, is the low cost of education, as compared to that in other cities, and the relative ease in obtaining visas. In 2017, Montreal was conferred the distinction of being the 'best student city in the world' by QS Rankings, leaving Paris and London lagging behind. With Trump to the south and Brexit across the pond, as it were, Canada is emerging as a coveted destination for international students; and Montreal has taken the top spot for its welcoming vibes, the geographical and racial diversity of its students, and its arts and culture scene. According to QS, the city also enjoys the privilege of being home to three of the best universities in the world: McGill, Concordia and Université de Montréal. But despite all that the city has to offer, Mohamad plans to leave it after his graduation.

'I'm not interested in staying in Montreal after graduation,' he declares. 'There is less scope here for jobs for international students. In Montreal, you must be bilingual – fluent in both English and French – to be hired. And employers here are looking for people with experience of having worked in Canada.'

If not Montreal, where would he prefer to go after graduation, I ask. His face lights up with the confidence that comes from certainty. There is only one destination in his mind: Vancouver.

'Very much Vancouver,' he says. 'There, weather, jobs – everything is better.'

In Vancouver, he has heard, the pay is better than in other cities, even for part-time work for university students. Here, at his job in Montreal, he earns $11 per hour, but he's been told that in Vancouver, an equivalent job would easily fetch him $15 per hour.

'That's really a lot of money for students,' he says.

Mohamad hasn't yet visited the city, but he knows Vancouver is the place for him. The hope of better pay and an improved lifestyle is prompting him to move from one end of the country to the other without a moment's hesitation. It was what had brought him to Canada in the first place. When I ask him about his motivation for coming to this country, he pauses and smiles.

Lapsing into Hindi, he confesses, 'It was always my dream to do my Master's in Canada or in the US.'

But although he acknowledges India's sound education system, Mohamad rues the fact that students there can earn no more than ₹20,000 to ₹30,000 a month.

'That's not enough for students to survive on,' he says regretfully.

While we're engaged in conversation, a woman strides into the store, her head held high, as though she owns the place. She is wearing dark sunglasses and a handbag dangles from her wrist. It turns out that she is, in fact, the owner or, at least, the manager. Looking me up and down as I stand by the till, writing in my notepad, she leans in to Mohamad and, without hesitation, cuts into my conversation with him.

Speaking in coarse Punjabi, she snaps, 'Don't speak to strangers. Why are you wasting your time with her? You can't trust anyone, you know. You really don't need to speak to her.'

She has no idea, of course, that I understand Punjabi. She turns to look at me again and flashes me a fake smile. I respond with a polite half-smile and move away, wandering the aisles and killing time so that I can resume my conversation with Mohamad after she has left.

Minutes later, the door shuts behind her. I look at Mohamad and roll my eyes.

'She is not so bad,' he says with an indulgent laugh.

I smile back. Watching her outside the window, I comment that while it is sunny outside, it is freezing cold.

He agrees. '*Kal* – 25 *tha, bahut* cold *tha.*'

Enduring such extreme weather and coming to grips with a foreign language, it's been a daunting challenge for Mohamad to discover and adapt himself to Montreal's quirks, but that's the whole point of going to university, isn't it? Expanding your horizons, stretching your boundaries, going beyond the tried and tested, the familiar and the comfortable, and discovering yourself anew – that is what makes the university experience, especially in a new country, so transformational.

Commenting on the most significant difference in learning goals and methods in Canada, as opposed to those in India,

Mohamad says, 'Here, I'm getting [acquiring] knowledge on how to communicate with people. Studying is different here. The methodology is totally different. In India, it is all about theory. Here, assignments are geared to achieving practical goals. We do projects on everything. We learn; we don't just memorize. And they check for plagiarism here. They even have open-book exams, which sound easy, but actually, it's very hard.'

Most of his fellow students are from Hyderabad.

'There are seven of us,' he says. 'Staying with friends is so much fun! Studying abroad alone is not comfortable; it can be an isolating experience.'

When he first arrived in Montreal, Mohamad was apprehensive about being able to make it.

'For one week, I was totally lost. The weather was different, the culture was different. People just don't care [about others]. They care if they are from our native place; then they care.'

Finding a group of friends from India has made all the difference. When spending time with them, he doesn't have to worry about speaking correctly in French or even in English.

'If you speak in English with friends, they make fun of you and say, "Come on, *yaar*, speak in Hindi."'

It's a relief being with friends, he admits, because in their company, you can speak your own language and be yourself.

'Here, you have to learn French. It's a major criterion for everything. Learning a language is too difficult.' It's easier to learn a software language, he laughingly declares.

We are interrupted again, this time, by the ring of his mobile phone.

'Yeah, bro,' he says into the phone.

It seems from his responses to the caller that he has been roped in for plans of going out somewhere tonight.

Mohamad enjoys the bachelor life abroad, living and hanging out with friends. 'Carefree, spontaneous, totally free,' is how he describes it. 'If we want good biryani, we go to Toronto. That's three hours away, but we don't care. We just decide to go and drive there. We can rent a car and go anywhere. Life is excitement; you've got to enjoy it,' he quips, a huge grin on his face.

He misses his family, but living away from them is not unusual for him.

'All my siblings are educated,' he says with obvious pride. 'They all live abroad: one in Dubai, another in Qatar, then one in Ireland, one in London. They all moved to places where they got good jobs.'

For Mohamad, studying and working abroad is evidently the ultimate sign of success. Though there's little scope for him to find a job in Montreal after his graduation, he's still grateful for the chance to study abroad.

'I'm studying. I have a job. I can't say anything bad about Montreal.'

Soon, I am heading out to meet others in the city who are learning French and trying to settle in for the long term.

There are many places in the city where students can sign up for English and French classes, including the South Asian Women's Centre that caters specifically to the needs of women in the community. The centre serves women and families and has a mission to help women become independent, empowered individuals. Among the services it offers, one of the most important is the free English and French classes that are available for anyone who is interested in acquiring essential language skills.

Keen on obtaining diverse insights into the issues faced by immigrants in Montreal, I speak to a centre manager of Pakistani origin who also teaches English and provides support and guidance to immigrant women through their cases. When I first call Juvaria, I reach her voicemail. The recorded voice begins by speaking in French and follows it up by repeating the same words in English. When I try again later, Juvaria answers the phone herself with a greeting in French, before realizing that I will be interacting with her in English.

'Well, of course, French is the official language of Quebec,' she reminds me.

Having worked at the centre for over a decade, Juvaria has helped countless women caught in a range of distressing circumstances. Some women had arrived in Montreal as refugees; others were sponsored by families. Many had travelled here after their spouses found jobs in Montreal. Juvaria tells me about the support the centre offers to women who are going through difficult times in their lives: some are facing domestic abuse and need shelter or protection; others are seeking legal assistance for asylum or immigration. She particularly emphasizes the importance of empowering women through language skills.

'Without language, they can't get out of their homes; they get completely isolated,' Juvaria declares. 'It's important for them to learn the language to go grocery shopping, go to the doctor, take public transportation. Many of them are afraid they'll get lost in the city if they travel alone. Without learning the language, that fear will always stay with them. Language is the first step to gain autonomy.'

In Quebec, many women from South Asian backgrounds first sign up for spoken English classes.

'A lot of the women we see haven't been to school past primary school,' Juvaria tells me. Students, she explains, come to learn English as a gateway to learning French.

Having interacted with her and been exposed to an Asian woman's point of view on the urgency of acquiring language skills in a city where they serve as a mode of survival and help in the assimilation of immigrants into a new culture, I am eager for another perspective on the situation. So I seek an appointment with Julie Bergeron, vice principal of the Centre William-Hingston, a community centre in Park Extension that houses a library, a primary school and a language school for adults, which is located above the library. I head over to the community library where she has asked me to meet her.

I enjoy wandering around while I wait. I love libraries with their quiet power to inform and bind a local community together, even across multiple languages. As in any other library around the world, I see signs put up announcing local community events: a Valentine's Day show with singing and dancing; promotion for a Sugar Shack and a students' café; an invitation for students of the French school to practise reading aloud in the language by reading out stories to children. There is a schedule to accommodate storytelling sessions, workshops and performances, and opportunities for adult learners to practise their spoken French by attending a 'talk shop' with library staff.

The Park Extension community is proud of its 'multi-ethnic origins'. Multiculturalism is honoured at the library. At the entrance is a sound installation that welcomes visitors in 40 different languages and invites them to explore the world on the bookshelves. There, they'll find books in many languages: Spanish, Italian, Greek, Hindi, Punjabi, Urdu, Bengali, Tamil and Gujarati.

The centre, which serves the needs of the community in a myriad of ways, is regarded as something of a treasure. Here, courses geared for adult education are on offer, particularly, those set up for learning spoken French as a second language. On its website, the centre lays special emphasis on the importance of learning French for those wishing to live in the province. '…At the Centre William-Hingston,' it says, 'francization rhymes with integration; the learning of the French language is combined with the discovery of the community, its values, its traditions, and its heritage.' The centre's mission, as stated on the website, is 'to bring non-Francophone adult immigrants to participate fully in the society that welcomes them'.

Learning to speak French in this region is vital to integration and community unity, and Julie will, I expect, tell me more about the urgency of teaching French to non-francophone immigrants.

She is warm and welcoming when we meet, and as bright as some of the best teachers you've been blessed with in your life. Petite and athletic, she is full of energy and good cheer. Her melodic voice glides easily between French and English as we walk down the long blue corridors towards her office. As I sit across from her at her desk, she adjusts her square-framed glasses and smooths out her ponytail. Then she begins to tell me about the centre and the language school.

'I'd been a French language teacher for twelve years, before becoming the vice principal here,' she informs me, before clarifying, 'I am really familiar with immigration and with French-language schools, because I've always been working in such schools. There are six French-language schools in Montreal, but here, we have the largest number of Indian people, because we are in Park Extension and this is mostly where they are settling down.'

At the centre, a dozen language classes are held in the morning, while four to five classes are held in the evening. The centre has around 450 students learning French. This is not among the largest of such schools, Julie explains, but just an average-sized one.

'There are some schools with 700 students,' she points out.

The teachers at the centre she runs have, like their students, come from all over the world.

'They speak good French,' Julie goes on, 'but some are from Italy, Romania, all over... They have been living here for 30–40 years and their French is perfect, so they can teach.'

Having lived in Montreal for over 20 years herself, she is a witness to how the city has evolved over time.

'I came to Montreal for university and I now live just three kilometres from here,' she tells me. 'I really love Montreal. I'm passionate about my city.'

Living in the Park Extension area, she has seen the population shift across communities over the years. Once an area known for its Greek population, it is now home to a number of newly formed communities.

'Before, almost 70 per cent were from India or nearby countries, but now it's about 50 per cent,' Julie observes. 'Still a lot, but more and more people are coming from Maghreb and Syria and South America. Close to here, in Little Italy, we have more and more people from South America. That is pretty new in the last ten years.'

But in recent years, she adds, Park Extension has been known for the predominance of its Indian community.

What's drawing Indians to Montreal, I ask her.

'Some of them have relatives here. Some of them, they like the idea of speaking French. But I think, to be honest... people come here, because it's an easier process to come to Montreal than to go to the other provinces, because fewer people want to come here. Then they get trapped; they like it and they stay on. A lot of people will stay here for a few years and then they move on to Toronto or Vancouver; so it's a way in.'

Students at the centre enrol themselves for lessons in reading, writing and speaking French, but they are also taught about French–Canadian culture, which will help them to integrate into the local and wider community. It is vital for new immigrants in Montreal to grasp the basics of French and understand the local culture to allow easy assimilation. But at the heart of it all is a passion for the language.

'It's a part of the culture here to speak French,' Julie explains. 'You can get a job if you only speak English, but if you speak both English and French, you'll get a better job.'

Though it is clear to me that a working knowledge of French is a basic necessity here, it is founded on a love of the language. I ask Julie for her views on the importance of French to the Quebecois, on their fierce pride in the language.

'I am sure you can ask this question to everyone in Montreal and everyone will have a different answer,' she quips.

She goes on to explain, however, that while she agrees that the language is a part of the culture, she doesn't feel it's crucial to its existence; in fact, to move away from French would represent an evolution, like moving away from the practice of speaking Latin.

'But if some people need to learn to speak French for work, I would like to help them,' she continues. '...I don't like the idea that everybody *must* speak French. I want to encourage everyone to learn it, but I don't want to force people into doing so.'

Learning the vernacular, the local idioms, as it were, is an important part of joining the community and understanding the intricacies of daily life in a new language. For many first-generation immigrants who come to learn French at the centre, the driving motivation is the communication gap that their inability to understand the language creates with their own children who were born and raised in Montreal and are fluent in French, the medium of instruction at their schools. Being able to understand and speak the language allows parents to stay connected and maintain their close intimacy with their offspring.

I sense the urgency of their need, because it reminds me of a book I once read called *When in French: Love in a Second Language*, where the author, Lauren Collins, relates how she fell in love with a Frenchman and how, as their relationship developed, she discovered the nuances of expressing love in a new language. Collins describes a moment from her life where her partner wishes to express his feelings for her in his native language, for 'talking to you in English,' he says, 'is like touching you with gloves'. That line beautifully captures the intimacy that language allows and the power it has to capture the taste and feel of a moment.

'A lot of people come here for their kids,' Julie acknowledges, elaborating on the desire of parents to learn the local language to strengthen their bond with their children. 'We see this a lot. Some people, they have been here for six, seven, ten years. And now their kids speak French fluently, so they want to be able to understand them. School for children here is all in French, because we have people here from all over the world. We cannot teach in English or in Spanish; we have to teach in French.'

Students at the centre come from diverse backgrounds and have various language needs. There are beginners, who start at the centre at level zero. This is usually meant for people who can only speak in their native tongue and have no knowledge of either French or English. These students are taught the basics, the phonetics of the language and are encouraged to familiarize themselves with the letters and the sounds. Students, who have either lived in Montreal and are acquainted with English or one of the Romance languages or can speak English, along with their native language, will start at level one. This course also teaches the basics, but builds on the languages that the students are already familiar with. The classes place more emphasis on spoken and conversational French, to begin with, but the further the students progress, the more grammar they are taught, and the focus gradually turns to the written language.

'Most students are excited, especially at level zero,' Julie explains. 'Even if they're afraid, there are so many people like them. They feel like, yes, this is a place where they learn French, but it's a place where they can settle and make [establish] links and a network with other people just like them.

'A lot of them arrive alone or with their spouse and sometimes, I meet students who studied here ten years ago and they still keep in touch with their friends from the class.'

Julie is empathetic enough to understand that for the students who enrol here, there is much more to their participation in the classes than merely acquiring the skill of communicating in French. They take away other things too – friendships and connections and even a sense of belonging as members of a group. As someone who likes to be connected to the wider world, Julie knows that the school offers a lifeline to people who have moved to Montreal.

'I love to travel and I like to discover, and I also like that people from all over the world are coming here and want to discover my culture as well,' she goes on. 'And I want to help them. It's a big commitment to leave your country and come here. Most of them do not do it for themselves; they do it for their family and for their kids. I think the least that I can do is to help them as much as I can.'

Through their participation in the classes held at the centre, Julie observes the progress of the students as they start from level zero and make it all the way to advanced classes like level six. If you start from level one and continue till the end, it will take a year to reach level six. But for certain students, it can take longer, depending on their natural flair for languages and the degree of their familiarity with French when they enrol. While Julie notices the obvious transformation that students go through over a year of classes, they themselves are often less assured about their progress and feel they haven't achieved enough.

'It's the same for almost of all them,' Julie tells me. 'So many of them are reaching level six, which is really high, and they still feel like they are not speaking fluently enough. They are so hard on themselves; they judge themselves so much. A lot of them, when they start, they think they cannot pick up the language. It's all so impressive.

'They are working very hard to learn and a lot of them, especially our students at night [who enrol for the evening classes], they work during the day and they come here from 5:45 till 10 p.m., four nights per week, plus work, plus family. They come and they are still enthusiastic.'

Listening to Julie and learning from her observations and my own, I never fail to be awed by the initiative and spirit that so many immigrants demonstrate when moving to a new country; they endeavour to work hard and build their lives anew, learning unknown languages and adopting unfamiliar customs along the way so that they can raise a family in one culture through the language of another.

The classes taking place during my interview with Julie are drawing to an end. She estimates that they will be over in the next ten minutes and invites me to go and stand in the corridor with her so that I can chat with the students while they're on their way out.

We make our way to the entrance, where the many hallways lined with classrooms meet. We wait for the school bell to ring, announcing the end of the lessons. Notepad ready, I'm looking forward to interacting with as many students as I can before they leave the premises.

The bell rings at precisely 3.30 p.m. Students pour out of the classrooms and crowd the hallways, chattering in languages from all over the world. Men and women from Maghreb, Syria, China, Pakistan, India and elsewhere mingle in the corridor and wave to Julie on their way out into that cold Tuesday in February.

In the hustle of students mingling in the halls, with some of them greeting Julie with a friendly 'Bonjour', I manage to strike up a conversation with a few. I chat with a woman who tells me that she speaks English and Pashto at home, although her children are growing up with French and learning to communicate in it. She herself is eager to acquire the capability of communicating with them in that language and to grasp what they are saying to each other as well.

Another woman I approach tells me that she ended up in Montreal, because her husband had got a job here. She lives in Park Extension – most newcomers start here, she explains.

'It doesn't matter how educated or uneducated you are,' she continues, 'you can learn to speak French.'

I meet a woman named Kulbir and another named Sadia. Then there's the woman from Kolkata who wears a star-shaped nose pin. She volunteers that she has been living in Montreal for nearly ten years.

'When I first came here, it was very different,' she admits.

She was only sixteen then and had accompanied her sister to this country. On turning eighteen, she had finished high school and gone back to India to get married. Nearly a decade ago, she returned to Montreal, married and pregnant. She couldn't go to university. She speaks Hindi and Urdu and is now learning French.

'When you're learning French, you sometimes speak half in French, half in English,' she confesses. 'So when you think, sometimes, the word doesn't come to mind.'

Another woman I chat with tells me about her daughter. For the first three years of the child's life, the mother had spoken to her in their own language, Urdu, but when the girl began picking up English and French in school, she knew her daughter needed formal instruction in the languages of the new culture.

But the woman is firm about one thing: 'First, it's important to understand your mother tongue.'

She has tried, she says, to build a bridge to India for her children and visits the country with her family.

'But it's hard, because my daughter complains about things like dirty bathrooms.'

When I ask her if she would ever consider moving back to India, she pauses to reflect. I can see that she is 'stuck', as so many are, tied as much to her family back home as she is to her life here in Montreal.

'Here,' she finally says, 'you can live in peace. Everything is in order. There, everything is difficult, nothing is simple. You end up wasting a lot of time and money to do basic things.'

She talks about healthcare and how she trusts the pharmacists and doctors here, because there is a clear, legal process of doing things and everyone is accountable. Back in India, on the contrary, just about anyone can prescribe medicine for you or sell it over the counter, she says.

But the picture here in Montreal isn't entirely rosy, she admits. Here, you only socialize on Saturdays and Sundays. Friendships at school are confined within its boundaries. The woman acknowledges that she does have friends in the community, but it's not the same.

'Also, the weather,' she adds with a groan. 'You have to wear jackets all the time.' But then she smiles and adds, 'But equally in India, you can't survive in the summer; too many mosquitoes!'

In the silence that descends on the deserted centre as the language students leave, the woman's description of her dilemma, shared by so many other Indian immigrants who have chosen this region as their new home, continues to resonate in my mind.

It strikes me that it's mostly women who are forthcoming and confident enough to speak to me. I recall my conversation with Juvaria, who teaches English at the South Asian Women's Centre. She herself had moved to Montreal from Pakistan years ago and had encountered the same challenges new immigrants face today.

'Learning a new language is a long process. Both languages, English and French, require patience to learn. French takes even longer than English,' she had confessed to me when I met her.

Juvaria now switches seamlessly between English and French.

'It is not difficult now, but it was an issue in the beginning,' I remember her telling me. 'I only spoke English when I arrived and I had the same fears as the people learning the language now. I worried about finding a job, making [putting down] roots here, making friends here. But that was a long time ago. Now, Montreal is home.'

Notes

[1] Krumm, Hans-Jürgen and Verena Plutzar, 'Tailoring language provision and requirements to the needs and capacities of adult migrants', University of Vienna.

Antwerp, Belgium

Diamonds are Forever

As an American, I find it so satisfying to enjoy the freedom of hopping onto the Eurostar and zipping in and out of multiple countries in a matter of hours. It takes us less than three hours after leaving London to slice through the tip of France and make our way into Belgium, a dream getaway for lovers of fine chocolates and beer. But what has brought me to this tiny European country is diamonds – lots of them.

From its capital, Brussels, we take the local train to Antwerp Central, where we'll be spending the next few days in the city's diamond district. For more than 500 years, this port city has been a hub for the global diamond trade and, over the years, the business has been passed down through generations and cultures. Historically speaking, Antwerp is a diamond-polishing centre. In fact, a statue of Lodewyk van Bercken, one of the city's first diamond polishers from the sixteenth century sits atop the busy Meir Street. But today, Antwerp is the global centre of the diamond trade.

Stepping off the train and walking out of the station, we find ourselves instantly immersed in the ambience of what locals call the Square Mile. In the narrow streets of this locality, roughly covering a square mile, diamonds worth billions of dollars are traded every year. It is said that over 80 per cent of all rough diamonds in the world pass through expert hands in Antwerp, and many of those diamonds have made the journey via Indian hands.

I linger before the window displays of the many jewellery shops that line the streets. What should have been a brisk walk to my first interview in the city slackens into a laggardly pace as I move from window to window, dazzled by the displays, the juxtaposition of the modest and the exquisite. During my stay over the next few days, I'll try on a five-carat emerald-cut diamond ring, because...why not?

I am surprised, however, at how mundane everything in the area looks and how unassuming everyone here seems, considering that some of the most expensive jewels on the planet are the focus of the main business conducted here. The people on the streets are dressed down. No power suits are in sight; only jeans, leather jackets and the occasional trench coat. One would never guess from their appearance and demeanour that millions of diamonds pass through the doors of these buildings every year.

In the past, the diamond industry here was run primarily by men from the Jewish community, but over the last few decades, it's the Indians, specifically, Gujarati Jains, who have been enjoying tremendous success in Antwerp's diamond district where their presence is conspicuous.

We check into the Astoria Hotel, right next door to the State Bank of India in Antwerp. Down the block from us stands a travel agency that solely promotes travel to India on its display windows. Posters with travel deals on direct flights and tour packages to India are plastered everywhere. Across from our hotel is a curious sign that says: 'Hari Krushna'.

I am on my way to the Antwerp Diamond Centre, where I will learn more about the industry and the Indians who are its major players. Along the way, I pass the Shanti Shop convenience store, with a mannequin in the display window clad in nothing but a black sequinned sari, and the Annpurna and Aahar Indian restaurants that are convenient stops for quick vegetarian meals. They set me thinking that the 'Little India' areas in the US or the UK might have looked very much like this decades ago. There is a meeting of disparate cultures on these streets, a certain degree of co-existence, with offices known for their traditionally Jewish names, like Horowitz, Friedberg and Rubin, standing side by side to Indian institutions like the Bank of India and ICICI Bank.

After passing through a guarded door and the mandatory security check, I sit across a table with Christopher and Ahalya of the Antwerp Diamond Centre who explain what makes the city such a thriving hub for the diamond business and how it came to pass that so many Indians joined the trade here.

'There are 1,700 companies here which give work to about 35,000 people,' Christopher informs me.

Antwerp caters to the full spectrum of the diamond business, covering functions like buying and selling, insurance companies, tender houses which bring in diamonds from smaller mining outfits based all over the world, transportation companies like Brink's, and banking services, which a significant number of Indian banks are involved in providing.

'You get everything and it is all in these three little streets, which is really exceptional,' Christopher remarks.

The diamond district is a condensed hub which draws producers, manufacturers and retailers – ranging from the most renowned, like Tiffany's and DeBeers, to the smaller companies – to the area for business. Over the generations, the focus of the business here has shifted; Antwerp's identity has evolved from being a diamond-polishing centre to one primarily involved in trading.

'You still have polishers here, just not that many,' Christopher adds. 'That's where the Indians came in and took over; it was in the polishing aspect [that they specialized].'

When Indian traders entered the market in the 1960s, they focussed on buying rough diamonds in smaller sizes, which they would send on to polishing houses, mainly in Surat, Gujarat. Once the polishing process was over, the traders would bring the diamonds back to Belgium and sell them worldwide. In fact, the business model adopted by the Indian community of traders of buying the small stones here, sending them back to

India to be polished and then selling them globally proved to be a winning strategy. But what greases the wheels of the trade are the incredible family bonds forged between traders around the world. Truly, at the heart of the success of Indians in the diamond trade in Antwerp are the solid family structures based on blood ties that shore up their businesses.

Ahalya's family was among the first few traders with Indian antecedents to establish their business in Antwerp in the 1960s. It all started with her grandfather, Sunil, who joined the first Indians to arrive and settle in the area between the late 50s and early 60s.

Born into a family of silversmiths in India, Sunil was one of a brood of more than ten, his granddaughter tells me. When he, along with his brothers, decided to turn the focus of the family-owned business from silver to diamonds, the family members strategically spread themselves across the world, establishing a network across hotspots like Mumbai, Antwerp, London and other cities.

'We had kids here – [in] London, Germany, Hong Kong, the States as well. Everyone was doing something. That's how the centres were built,' Ahalya tells me.

This global network isn't unique to her family alone, she goes on. 'Everyone here has a cousin, a brother, an uncle somewhere around the world' whom they trade with. 'My family are in Bombay, Singapore, Dubai, New York, London... We are really everywhere. We are scattered around a lot.'

The strong family relationships and close-knit community in

Antwerp are quite evident. Here, everyone is bonded together by diamonds, Jain culture, deep ties with India and an ongoing chain of migration, whereby families already living here help to settle in newcomers and their families and bring them into the business. Over the next few days, I will learn more about this trend and observe it first-hand.

Ahalya's grandfather had come to Antwerp alone, leaving his wife and children behind in India, until he was settled enough to call for them a few years later. Two of his children were born in India; the others were born in Belgium after his wife and family joined him in 1964. As with many of the first generation of new settlers, Sunil's early days in Antwerp were tough.

'There wasn't really anything here [in those days],' Ahalya tells me. 'His stories are always about how he came here and he was the only vegetarian. For him, it was like a completely new world.

'At the beginning, [breaking into the] business was very hard. The history here was all Jewish and they [Indians] were alien people who came much later and were working in lower quality rough diamonds. They traded within the family, with their cousins in London or their cousins in Bombay. That's how it started,' she goes on to explain.

'Since then [subsequently], my father joined the business, and the plan is that my brothers will too. It is really all about the generations.'

She talks with pride and enthusiasm about her 'talented and capable' brothers, but I wonder if this smart young woman in her early twenties with exposure to the family business and experience in the diamond industry isn't keen on carving out a place for herself in this area by joining her male siblings in running the business. I'm curious about her own plans which I will discuss with her later, while also broaching the subject of Indian women leaders in the industry here.

From those early days when Ahalya's grandfather settled in Antwerp, the Indian community has grown from a mere five families into a thriving community, its members bound by an intricate network involving diamonds and shared links with India. Unlike the other Indian communities I've visited around the world, the one in Antwerp has retained its deep ties with India, so much so that even the generation of children born in Belgium have tangible connections with their homes and families back in India which they keep alive through their regular visits there all through the year.

'Most people go [to India] twice a year,' Ahalya observes. 'The mothers with little children will usually leave in July and [the] fathers will join [them] in August. They go for a month and a half and they'll come back to Belgium before the fasting period, which is at the end of August, usually.'

Even more popular than the summer vacations spent in India are the annual trips that are undertaken in December, when relatives and business partners scattered around the world come together.

'We all meet in December in Mumbai,' Ahalya tells me. 'All the families come together – the entire community from here and my cousins from all around the world as well. The group keeps getting bigger and bigger every year. Bombay in December, everyone is there!'

It's easy to understand how these robust global family ties have helped businesses go from strength to strength over the years. While the businesses in Antwerp have been evolving from the early days of their arrival, Indians in the industry have succeeded in establishing themselves as some of the key players in the diamond trade.

'Some of the biggest and most prestigious companies, most of them are now Indian, I would say,' Christopher declares.

Later that evening, after my interview and meeting with him and Ahalya are over, my husband and I settle into the city as we walk from the diamond district down to Antwerp's Grote Markt, a classic picture postcard-worthy European market square that dates back to mediaeval times. With its cobblestone streets, central town hall and the colourful façades of its multi-storeyed buildings, this is a tourist's delight and we take our time sampling local beers at each of the pubs we visit. Among them is one that proudly offers a range of 300 different beers to choose from.

We spend a few hours making our way around the square and end up having dinner at a Thai restaurant. For a city that has a significant population of Indians in business, we don't see very many Indian restaurants beyond the peripheries of the diamond district. Nor do we notice many Indians frequenting the many bars around the place. With the majority of them belonging to the Jain faith, it is clear to an idle observer that they are not exactly hanging out at the local pubs. Wondering where the local Indian community lives and does, in fact, hang out, we set out in the morning to find them.

Our taxi drops us off in the parking area just outside the Antwerp Jain temple, also called the Jain Cultural Center. Situated in that area of the city known as Wilrijk, a well-manicured neighbourhood that is home to several Indians and is roughly a fifteen-minute drive from the diamond district, the cultural centre, in the eyes of many local Indians, is what keeps the community together, serving as the hub of religious and cultural activity throughout the year.

On our way from the diamond district to the Jain Center, we pass through neighbourhoods inhabited by Hasidic Jews; all dressed in black outfits and hats, they are either walking or cycling with their children. The closer we get to the temple, the fancier the houses become. Not that people here are inclined towards a show of opulence. On the contrary, wealthy though they are, their lifestyle is understated. We do, however, notice the occasional home with the names of the owners inscribed on the outside or with writing in Hindi displayed above the gates.

On reaching the cultural centre, we walk through the parking area which is packed with Audis, MiniCoopers, Mercedes and

BMWs. This is clearly a prosperous community, but there's no overt manifestation of affluence. You hardly come upon any nameplates boasting first names or family names. As we approach the temple entrance, it is clear that the crowds of people present here have not come to visit the house of worship, but to go elsewhere.

From the side of the temple, loud cheers and the unmistakable, infamous, piercing tune of IPL cricket's trumpeting burst forth. Adjacent to the temple stands the Antwerp Indian Cricket Club which, I will come to learn later, is an older building. Cricket first, is usually the priority. Crowds roar when a ball is hit and flies out into the carpark. The Bollywood song, 'Tamma Tamma,' blasts out through loudspeakers to celebrate a sixer. The IPL trumpet tune blares on repeat. We turn away from the temple entrance and approach the cricket grounds, passing a group of little boys and girls who are playing their own versions of a cricket match on a vacant patch of grass.

It's a big day on the cricket grounds, marking the third year of the Antwerp Indian Premier League championships. This annual tournament brings together 150 participants who, divided into ten teams, compete against each other. The participants are all locals, all Indians, and all working in the diamond trade.

It is estimated that over the next three days, a thousand people will participate in the tournament, either as team members or as spectators. This is quite clearly an impressive event, with professional-looking cricket kits and formal teams proudly bearing names like the Blue Gems, Antwerp Badshahs, Rising

Kings, KGK Royals, Indian Warriors, Maroon Challengers and even Dabang Swintu Stars.

On the side of the pitch, I meet a young woman named Pooja. She is sitting on a bench in the shade of a large tree. By her side is her husband, a player for one of the teams. Also sharing the bench with them are their two young daughters whom she painstakingly feeds with bites from a home-made paratha. As we get talking, Pooja informs me that she arrived here from Mumbai eight years ago.

'Except for the weather, everything is the same,' she quips, laughing.

She acknowledges that as a newcomer to the city, she felt reassured by the close-knit local Indian community living here and looked upon its members as an extended family that not only provided her much-needed social and emotional support, but even helped bring up her children in the culture to which she herself had been born and bred.

'At home, we speak Gujarati and English,' she confides, 'but they [her children] go to a local Dutch school.'

We move on and find a seat in the second row of the stands among the families supporting the teams. Everyone is wearing branded shirts and proudly supporting their favourite teams. This is a family day out and the stands are full of men and women of all ages. The 'aunties' in the stands are the loudest in their response to the match in progress, their eyes carefully following the game as they take stock of every run taken and every movement of the ball.

I jump down from the stands to mingle with the milling crowd and meet a friendly woman named Saloni who tells me that next year's tournament will be more exciting still – they have formed a Women's Cricket League with seven teams to which an eighth may soon be added. They plan on competing at next year's tournament, she adds with unmistakable pride. She reminds me of Ahalya. I wonder if Indian women living here are coming forward to make their presence felt both in the diamond business and within the community.

Saloni explains that the members of the local Indian community come together to participate in activities all through the year and not just for the cricket tournament that takes place in spring. During the winter months, which can be cold and damp in Antwerp, they play games that can be held indoors, like badminton and bowling, forming teams and hosting tournaments for those sports as well. And, of course, during the festival months, they come together to celebrate Navrati, Diwali, Ganpati, Holi and more.

Saloni herself had arrived in Antwerp nearly ten years ago following an arranged marriage to a non-resident Indian who lived here. Initially shocked when she discovered that she'd be moving to Belgium after her wedding, she has settled in well, she admits.

'Any new place is difficult at first,' she goes on. 'The language and the food were the hardest [to adapt to].'

In Antwerp, the Belgian locals speak a mix of languages – English, Dutch and Flemish. But the city's Indian community now lives mostly around Wilrijk (Saloni explains that the 'j' is pronounced like a 'y'), the area near the temple.

What helped her to settle in when she was a newcomer, she informs me, was the growing Indian community.

'Now there are so many people,' she observes.

She's glad she has somewhere to take her parents when they come over to visit from India – the temple and the cultural centre have so much to offer the community.

While we're in mid-conversation, a small child, probably her youngest, approaches her. Saloni proceeds to feed her bits of jalebi even as she continues chatting with me and volunteers that her children go to a Dutch school like the other locals.

I say good-bye to her and move on. As I stroll through the grounds, I realize that I'm among youngsters who might possibly be considered the 'cool' crowd – young and strikingly good-looking teenagers, all sitting in a row of the stands near the back of the pitch. They come across as smart, warm, funny adolescents who have all grown up together in Antwerp. Many of them attend the International School here and can speak English and Dutch as well as Gujarati.

'Most of us can't read or write Gujarati, but we all speak it at home,' they tell me with candour.

When I ask where they feel more at home, in India or in Belgium, they all reply, 'Both.' I learn that many of them travel back to India at least twice a year and that for them, the transition involved in moving between two homes, countries and cultures is apparently seamless.

I continue meeting those who have come to watch the cricket match and enjoy engaging in conversation with many of the locals.

'India has changed,' they declare.

'When we came [to Belgium] 40 years ago, India was a different place; there was so much poverty,' says a local who has lived in Antwerp for the last few decades and describes how the diamond business in the city has grown as much as the business in Surat and Mumbai has.

Bobby Low, a charming older man and native Belgian, has been observing over a period of time the influx of Indians and the growth of the community in Antwerp. When I first approach him to ask if he is here for the cricket, he replies, 'I'm here, because I have many friends here.'

I can well believe that, because even as I'm speaking to him, people come up to hug and greet him with a 'Hello, Bobby *bhai*.'

I'm looking for any form of tension that might exist under the surface, but all I sense is genuine warmth in the interactions between members of this community, along with a feeling of serenity. Today is truly a wholesome family day out for local Indians.

We are invited to join the crowd in a massive tent behind the cricket pitch where food is being served. We do so gladly, smelling the aromas emanating from there. But as is typical of most Indian functions, be it at home or abroad, the niceties fall by the wayside as soon as it's time to queue up for the food. In no time at all, it has become an exercise in the survival of the fittest as we all jostle to get through the doors and into the hall where the food is laid out. We queue up patiently, but all around us, people push and shove to get through. There's much light-hearted banter as people try to jump the queue and talk their way through, badgering the poor guy in charge of crowd control at the doors. Once we make it inside, we're queuing up again to be served from a wide array of dishes. All through the process, I'm being pushed and prodded by a short, bespectacled woman standing directly behind me who smiles every time I turn to give her a withering look, but continues to prod and poke me, nonetheless.

At long last, we are served a thali of fresh, piping hot Jain vegetarian food.

'This has onions; this doesn't,' we're told as the servers pile everything from *daal-bhat* to pesto pasta on our plates. To put it simply, every item is delicious. We wash it all down with a tall glass of savoury lassi. Once again, I queue up for the lassi, but by now, my husband is wiser; he jumps the queue to pour us a few glasses.

Later, we are allowed to visit the temple and explore its interiors. But since neither my husband nor I are Jains, we are cautioned against getting too close to the *murtis*. Judging, however, by the disapproval expressed by a man at the door over our entry, it is clear that we're lucky to be allowed into the temple in the first place.

Inside, the temple is immaculate, with traditional designs and motifs hand-carved into marble and wood. I learn that the marble was imported and chiselled here on site over many years by workers who are especially brought in from India for six months at a time for that very purpose. Graceful arches curve overhead and the ceiling soars up into majestic domes, while beneath our feet is the cool stone floor to ground devotees. Quiet worshippers – elders, mothers, children – make their way around the area, navigating the sacred space with care, praying softly to express their individual devotion for each of the deities represented there.

We leave the main hall and wander through the temple's vast grounds, finding our way to a magnificent cultural hall, guarded by tall, intricately carved wooden doors. The hall can accommodate 600 people and I can well imagine the community's most important functions taking place in this space. Just passing through it is akin to wandering through one of those great, immaculately maintained havelis of India – calm, peaceful, awe-inspiring.

As we stroll around the place, we meet Sapna, a warm and welcoming local who has much to tell us about the bustling activity inside the temple.

'Antwerp is auspicious,' she announces with a beaming smile. She goes on to explain that most of the local Indian children come here for Sunday school. 'Everyone lives within a 20-mile radius,' she adds.

Her own six-year-old can run around freely without her worrying about his whereabouts, because everyone here knows everyone else.

'We all look out for each other and for each other's children,' she tells me, going on to express her preference for religious ceremonies held in Antwerp, rather than back in India. 'It's [such ceremonies are] not fragmented in Antwerp; everyone comes together.'

India has changed so much, she complains. People are always on edge and there's so much traffic out there that it's hard to plan the day and get things done.

We tour the library area, furnished with giant wheeled chairs so that the kids can come together or sit individually and study. The children's *pathshala* exam is coming up soon and they are all eager to pass, because every one of them is keen on performing in the upcoming play and the right to do so is conditional: they have to pass their exams to be eligible. Just as the adults fast together, the children study and play together at the temple.

I cannot help being moved by the warmth of the people in the temple, by their apparent inclusiveness, which seems to suggest that everyone is part of one big family. But I wonder if any interracial weddings have ever taken place within this community, and sense that something like that might be considered an aberration serious enough to rock this homogenous group of people united by language, religion and, of course, diamonds.

'When in Antwerp, look closely at the ground when you walk; you might find a diamond.'

That is a tip we pick up from our tour at Diamond Land, one of the larger showrooms in the diamond district. From then on, I am extra mindful of where we step.

We walk across the small square dotted with international diamond centres, trading houses called bourses, and insurance firms. All around us, men – Gujarati, Jewish and others – are hurrying off somewhere, carrying black leather briefcases. My thoughts go back to Ahalya; I wonder how this scene might change in the coming years, as a new generation of intelligent young women like her, keen to work in the family business and in diamonds, begins to emerge in more prominent roles.

As I continue on my way, keeping a careful eye on the concrete for the slightest hint of sparkle, I hear a loud 'Kaimcho!' ring out from across the street. I look up to see a businessman running to meet an acquaintance of his. They shake hands and break into Gujarati, communicating in that language until another man, who is obviously not an Indian, joins the conversation.

Something that Christopher had said during our interview comes to mind. 'The cultures here pretty much stick with each other, but if you are doing business here, then you'd better forget your culture quickly, because it is all about the deal, period. If you have a problem with somebody's culture or background, then you shouldn't be here. You are not going to do business.' In fact, that's the model in Antwerp, according to him. 'Outside, you see a big sign on the street; it says, "In Antwerp, we speak diamond."'

'It is funny,' Ahalya remarks, 'because working in the trade, you use words adapted from both cultures. For example, "*mazelais*" the Hebrew word that you would use to conclude a good deal is used by Indians too.'

Ahalya is fluent in the language of diamonds. It's no exaggeration to state that she and her two brothers grew up surrounded by diamonds. From a young age, the three of them were exposed to the workings of the family business and participated in the operations in whatever way they could.

'On a Wednesday, which was a half-day at school, I'd run with my backpack to my Dad's office and get super-excited that I would get to touch these stones,' Ahalya recalls.

In those early days of her involvement with the family business, her contribution was confined to sitting under her father's desk and finding all the little stones that had spilled on the floor.

'They were all real diamonds, but all very, very small,' she remembers with a laugh. 'But it was just that excitement – to come to the office and see, "Oh, both my father and my grandfather are doing it."'

Searching for the stones that might have fallen and scattered on the floor would turn into a competition with her brothers as the children scoured the ground to find the odd runaway diamond.

'As we grew older – I think I was coming up [to the] second grade, so I was seven or eight – I was actually counting stones. That's really how we learned "to count", and my dad taught us at a very young age how to get excited about it. We would get 100 stones and then count them like a trader would count them – by batches of four. You collect five batches of four stones each time – so a pile of 20 – and then we would realize, 'Okay, you've got five batches now. Each of them [has] 20 stones. You've got 100.'

Practising her multiplication tables by counting and sorting batches of diamonds and then organizing them into neat sets wrapped in parcel paper, exactly in the way that traders carry diamonds, constituted Ahalya's first experience of adding value to the family business. With time, she would learn about the colours, then the different shades of diamonds and eventually gain exposure to the commercial side of the business. All this she picked up from her father, who would make the business seem accessible to all his children.

'It was always done in a way where you felt like you were doing something important,' Ahalya now acknowledges. 'It's just really cool to have that exposure at such a young age, because a lot of my friends [whose families were in the same business] weren't necessarily that interested in it. But for us, there was always something to be excited about.'

With such early exposure to the business and their acquaintance with so many families in the same trade, diamonds for Ahalya, as for many of the Jain families in Antwerp, have come to serve as the common thread that runs through their global lives. 'All our friends, all our cousins are just sort of part of it. Even travel-wise, all our holidays were based on where the business would be; and that way, we'd meet people and cousins. I think in a way, it [diamonds] makes it feel like home.'

Unlike many of the younger generation of Indians living in Antwerp, who studied at the local International School, Ahalya attended a local Belgian Catholic school, learning to speak the local Flemish language before she did English.

'I think I was six years old when I first noticed that I wasn't like everyone else around me,' she reminisces. 'Everyone was Belgian, but [in addition] we had things like religious classes that my parents made us attend on Sunday to learn the Jain culture and learn all the prayers that you're supposed to know. And that was the first time when I was like, "Oh, there is a culture. There is something else. There are two parts to us – a Belgian part of me, but there's also this Indian part."'

There were moments of confusion, but no existential identity crisis as such, she now acknowledges, 'because my dad always told us that you're both'.

Ahalya went to London for her university studies, along with 35 of her contemporaries from the Antwerp Indian community. There, she specialized in Marketing Communications, an area she enjoys working in even now. Before she considers joining her own family business one day, Ahalya is gaining traction in her career and gathering experience in the industry by working elsewhere. And she's not the only young woman looking to join an otherwise male-dominated sector within the community.

'Women are now going to Surat to learn about polishing, which is not something that was acceptable a few years ago.

Now there are a lot more girls who are breaking the barriers and saying, "Well, we were exposed, we went to the international schools, we went to university." There is no difference anymore. There are definitely more women [in the diamond business], which makes it exciting.'

Ahalya actively engages in the growing local chapter of the Women's Jewellery Association, a networking organization for women in the trade, that represents not just those of Indian origin, but also Belgians, Lebanese and women from all over the world who work in Antwerp.

It is apparently from her grandfather, the original visionary who brought them into the diamond industry in Antwerp, that Ahalya has received encouragement to advance in her chosen career.

'In 10 years,' she declares confidently, 'I'll still be here.'

Dubai, UAE

DOWN THE AISLE

It is a relief to shed the multiple layers of winter, change into outfits made from lighter and more porous fabrics and let my skin revel in Dubai's April heat. We stay for a few days, soaking in the sun by Jumeirah Beach and enjoying the over-the-top luxe surroundings of some of Dubai's tourist hotspots. From gilded elevators to sharks gliding by in aquariums, I can see for myself why the place is known as a playground for the world's billionaires. But revelling in the luxuries on offer is not part of our current plans; we're setting off from one desert oasis and heading for another.

Travelling in a bus from Dubai to Abu Dhabi, we're looking forward to attending a family wedding in the capital city. It is a destination wedding arranged for a couple who live in London, but chose to celebrate their nuptials with guaranteed sunshine as a backdrop. The traffic flows swiftly on the palm tree-lined highways and in less than two hours, we're there. We realize that we are approaching Abu Dhabi as we see signs advertising

Ferrari World and get a distant glimpse of the stunning white domes and minarets of the Grand Mosque.

Our bus nears the gates and the long drive leading up to the newly inaugurated Ritz Carlton Hotel, where the wedding festivities will play out over the next several days. Alighting from the bus, we are greeted by a *dhol* player, who drums away on the instrument for at least ten minutes without a break, as we dance our way into the hotel where the wedding parties are lined up to welcome us. They aren't alone; guests of the hotel come down as well to watch the boisterous procession, and the hotel staff are on hand to welcome us with garlands and fresh cups of mint tea.

We had known from the minute we heard that Vikas and Selina were planning a destination wedding in Abu Dhabi that this occasion would be a special one. But it is only when we arrive at the hotel that it strikes us: over the next few days, an unforgettable experience is in store for us.

Everything associated with this wedding is larger than life. Friends and family from around the world have flown in for the celebrations and every detail is accounted for. From an evening garden party and a Vegas-themed sangeet to an open-air Hindu wedding ceremony, this wedding is picture-perfect from start to finish.

Selina, who grew up within the Sindhi community in London, knew she wanted a destination wedding from the moment her fiancé proposed to her.

'I wanted the wedding to be in the Middle East because of

134

the service – I wanted everyone to have that royal treatment that you can only get in the Middle East,' Selina now declares. 'We also wanted a place that could cater to an Indian wedding. That's why we couldn't look at Europe; they don't understand Indian concepts.'

'I wanted somewhere that understands the culture, a place where they understand what is a *mandap*, what is a puja, what are all these terms.'

The glittering Middle Eastern cities off the coast of the Persian Gulf are today's hot spots for Indian destination weddings, rivaling locations like Bali and Thailand. *Vogue India* says, 'Located just three hours away from India in a serendipitous midway mark, the region is a cultural crossroads with grandeur, opulence and a global-local flavour to match the new-age Big Fat Indian Wedding.'

It's not just weddings of non-UAE residents that fill the resort calendars here. Indian weddings account for big business in the UAE, where some three million Indian émigrés, representing the largest population of Indian émigrés in the world, live. Mostly from Kerala and other south Indian states, Indians account for a substantial percentage of the total population in the UAE, with their cultural influence evident across the emirates. It's no surprise, then, that Dubai's famed gold souks see a surge in sales during the Indian wedding season, with not just local Indians flocking to them, but also those who consider it worth their while to travel all the way from India so that they can avail of the significantly lower prices on which no sales tax is levied by

Dubai's administration. The average wedding in the UAE can cost close to US $80,000, a sum that several Indian families are ready to spend. But it isn't necessarily only in the UAE that the cost of Indian weddings has skyrocketed.

The spectacular weddings organized by members of the Indian diaspora today are a recent phenomenon witnessed over the past few decades. In the UK, for example, research undertaken in 2015 on the subject by Asian wedding magazines indicates that the average British Asian wedding in that country costs upwards of £50,000, more than twice the amount expended for the average UK wedding, which costs around £21,000. Estimates of the expense incurred in organizing Indian weddings on a more modest scale come in around £25,000 – which still exceeds the average cost of a British wedding.

But it wasn't always so. Hardly a few decades ago, the first emigrants to Indian-diaspora countries across Africa, Europe and North America would make do by organizing weddings in their homes or in makeshift halls rented for the purpose.

'There's a lot more pressure nowadays to organize an extravagant wedding,' Selina tells me. 'Social media puts so much pressure. What to do at each event, what gift hampers to give out, what items to put into each hamper. Then there's the decor and the seating plan. I don't imagine our parents had to deal with such complicated seating plans! And related to the seating plan, what about the chairs? What are the chairs going to look like? It's about going down to the minutest detail for everything.'

Waiting for the elaborate *baraat* to arrive at a wedding I attended recently, I remember hearing an older guest say, 'Where was all this in our day? We never had this when we got married. Our weddings were so simple, then.'

My own parents in the US have similar memories. 'We were married in my brother-in-law's home,' says my mother.

'We were married above the corner shop our family ran,' my husband's parents in the UK recall.

But that was decades ago.

Today, Indian couples – mostly, second-generation Indians – plan their perfect nuptials with meticulous attention to the details, taking into consideration both Indian tradition and current trends from their home country. From the UAE and America to the UK, venues are judiciously selected, keeping in mind the ambience of the place, the status it enjoys in the public imagination and the capacity it has to hold large numbers of guests, running into the hundreds. An entourage of wedding professionals assists in creating full-blown wedding mega events. Mehndi artists, make-up artists, hairstylists, tailors, florists, decorators, caterers, cake bakers, wait staff, videographers, photographers, *dhol* players, deejays, venue managers, planners, chauffeurs, horse minders and more, all play a role as part of the growing production crews behind some of the large-scale Indian weddings that have become the norm all over the world. I even know of a wedding which shut down the streets of Washington, DC, to allow the groom to arrive his wedding atop an elephant. With a growing Indian wedding industry that is already valued at well over £300 million a year in the UK alone, there is no sign of these trends downsizing.

The increasing size and trappings of Indian weddings around the world and the expenditure they involve can be linked to the overall growth in population of the Indian community worldwide as well as to an overall increase in the wealth enjoyed by its members. A robust competitive spirit also contributes, no doubt, to the surging popularity of bigger and more elaborate weddings. Across cultures and throughout the world, weddings are becoming glitzier and of longer duration, with higher production values and a greater celebrity feel. There is, nonetheless, something culturally unique about the widespread compulsion to establish how 'Indian' such weddings really are these days.

The majority of weddings I attend are organized to celebrate the union of couples who were born to Indian parents and brought up in England or America. At most of these weddings, the couples, who have but a tenuous link with their roots in India, choose to celebrate the occasion by observing Indian religious rituals and being faithful to their ancient cultural traditions.

Selina puts it best while describing her own response to the different aspects of her wedding: the civil ceremony, on the one hand, and the traditional rites and festivities that followed it.

'The civil ceremony was exciting. But I only felt half-married,' she confesses with a laugh.

In fact, Selina and Vikas celebrate both anniversaries,

commemorating their civil wedding and the traditional one.

'I regard both occasions as [deserving of celebration as] an anniversary,' Selina declares. 'But I place more significance on the Indian wedding; we are Indian, after all. When we dream, we don't dream in white. I never dreamt about walking down the aisle in white. I dreamt in red and that I'm walking towards a mandap. The civil ceremony is exciting and we do celebrate it, but we do it for legal reasons.'

I wonder if future generations will continue to marry in this way, when they don't necessarily have the same immediate links to India as we do as second-generation children of the diaspora. What does it all mean, I ask myself.

That the trend of organizing elaborate Asian weddings is not confined to the United Arab Emirates, and is just as popular beyond it is something I am reminded of while attending another beautiful wedding back in London. Priti, a friend of the family, had married her sweetheart, Anil, in an elaborate ceremony that would stretch over weeks.

Both bride and groom were born and raised in England. Each of them speaks English with a distinct accent – Anil's twang from Manchester and Priti's from Essex. They were introduced by a mutual friend. After a series of dates, photos of the two snuggling together started appearing on her Facebook page. It was official; they were in love.

Priti and Anil's civil wedding took place in the spring. While the ceremony marked their legal marriage, like other Asian couples in the UK, the pair decided to have a separate, religious Hindu wedding ceremony to officially bind the marriage. After the formalities had been completed on the day of their civil ceremony, they hosted a party for a few hundred guests under a garden marquee on the grounds of a stately manor in Essex, but they referred to the occasion as their 'engagement'.

'At the civil ceremony, I did feel married, but only for a few minutes,' Priti would confide later. 'After the ceremony, I felt exactly the same; only now I had a ring on my finger and a certificate. Things just went back to the way they were.'

Later that night, Priti and Anil were seperated by distances again when Anil returned to his home in Manchester and the couple were back to speaking to each other on the phone every night. It was the traditional Indian wedding that Priti had been eagerly waiting for.

It was the traditional Indian wedding that she had been eagerly waiting for.

'It's what I've seen all my life. It's what I grew up imagining for my own wedding,' she acknowledged. 'I've even attended weddings in India, although it's funny – they try to be Westernized in their weddings, while we try to be traditional.' The irony prompted a laugh. 'Maybe, for us, it's the novelty of doing something different from our daily life, doing it in an Indian way.'

What Priti was looking forward to the most was the *chura*

ceremony, which would take place on the morning of her Indian wedding. On this occasion, her maternal uncles would help her put on the customary glittering red and white bangles that many north Indian brides wear at their wedding and for weeks afterwards as a symbol of being newly married. For Priti, the red bangles represented the ultimate identity of a bride and were more meaningful for her than the white dress she had worn to her civil ceremony.

'To me, wearing the *chura* represented that I was getting married,' she would tell me later. 'When I first put them on, I just couldn't stop looking at them.'

Priti is a pharmacist, but it seems to her now that in the months running up to her big day, planning her wedding had become a priority and taken over as her full-time job. She knew what she wanted, though. When she dreamed of her wedding day, she visualized it both as a grand Indian event, like the ones in the Bollywood movies she watches, and as an occasion like the ones in the UK that she had attended all her life. She also knew that for her civil ceremony, she would wear a white dress and have bridesmaids in attendance on the day. In a way, by having both a civil ceremony and a traditional Indian wedding, Priti got the best of both of her worlds.

For Priti's parents, who were married in a quiet ceremony in the UK, it was the chance to gift the wedding of their dreams – the grand wedding celebration they had never had – to their daughter.

'She's our only daughter. It's our duty,' her father had told me.

'The wedding is about fulfilling not just my dreams, but their dreams too,' Priti would add later.

But where is the vision of the 'dream Indian wedding' coming from?

For Priti, the source was a mix of Bollywood movies and the Indian television programmes that air on Indian satellite channels being beamed into homes around the world.

'I started watching those serials with my mum, probably about five or six years ago. That's when I started dreaming of having a traditional Indian wedding and the fairy-tale big, happy Indian family,' she recalled, adding that the other contributing factor was *Asiana*.

Priti was referring to *Asiana Wedding*, a UK-based bridal magazine which describes itself as 'the iconic bridal Bible' and the 'biggest Asian fashion magazine in the world'. As is also the case with non-Indian weddings, it is bridal magazines like this one that lead the way in creating visions of that 'one perfect day'. The quarterly, which is available digitally, is entirely devoted to the needs of Indian brides who live outside India, but is also sold in India, as well as in sixteen other countries. *Asiana Wedding* magazine is the most popular of its kind in the UK, followed by others like *Asian Bride*. Other internationally available magazines like *South Asian Bride* cater to their target local readership. These glossies fill their pages with South Asian-style bridal eye candy. On the cover of its Autumn 2017 issue, *Asiana Wedding* promises 'everything you need for the biggest day of your life', while another headline offers 'bold and beautiful bridal looks for 2018' inside. In an earlier issue of the same magazine, an editorial had described the latest evolution of the Indian wedding: '...The smaller scale Asian wedding has become *de rigueur,* with banqueting suites being replaced by manor halls, stately homes and even art galleries. Finally, we are seeing Asian weddings that are a far cry from the chaos of yesteryear and are turning into sophisticated, easy to manage affairs.'

I beg to differ on one point: of the dozens of Indian weddings I've attended in the past few years, none of them have been 'smaller scale' by any stretch of the imagination. If anything, they are growing in scale, detail and precision. But it is true that they have evolved from the loosely planned events that would take place in school gyms and local recreation centres decades ago. But those weddings are some of my favourite childhood memories. I fondly remember attending weddings as a child, when my large extended family would gather together in each other's homes. My cousins and I would sleep in the basement, huddled under blankets or curled up in sleeping bags, while our parents would sleep in spare bedrooms or on sofas in living rooms. We would take turns putting mehndi on each other's palms, dipping toothpicks into bowls of wet henna to draw simple designs like flowers and smiley faces. Food would be cooked at home and everyone would help with the arrangements. Nothing ever started on time and nothing ever finished without long, heartfelt farewells.

Now, wedding guests are accommodated in hotel rooms across town and events are coordinated by well-paid wedding planners. Weddings are lavish and pre-planned to the last painstaking detail, as if lifted straight out of a magazine photo shoot. While these weddings can be a beautiful reflection of abundance, I miss the charm and closeness that backyard weddings allow.

With an ever-growing Indian global wedding industry, there is always someone to cater to a bride's every need, every whim. Magazines have pages of wedding fashions for the 'modern Indian bride' who has more control over her wedding arrangements today than did her counterparts from previous generations who lived in a time when weddings were often left to the parents to manage. The Indian bride today is empowered to not only choose her groom, but manage most aspects of her special day, ranging from budgets to guest lists, while still connecting with her Indian culture. Some brides have gone further and written about 'sexist wedding traditions that need to be modernized', including the practice of the bride's family bearing the burden of the costs and the ceremonial 'giving away' of their daughter during the *kanyadan* ritual.

At Priti's wedding, I remember meeting her in the bridal suite. She sat there stoically, a heavy beaded silk veil, easily weighing five pounds, draped carefully over her hair. Dazzling gems hung from her ears, hugged her neck and rested in the parting of her hair and on her forehead. Her hair had been fashioned into an immaculate bun and was held in place with dozens of crystal-studded pins. Her fiery orange wedding ensemble had thousands of diamantes hand-sewn into the fabric and a thick band of red and white bangles spiralled around her wrists. Even her feet, hidden under the flowing wedding dress, were decorated with henna patterns and a toe ring.

On her wedding day, there would be another outfit for Priti to wear in the evening. After the religious ceremony, she would change into an equally breathtaking gown in a muted coral for the reception, a modern take on her vibrant orange traditional morning attire, incorporating elements of Western design.

Waiting for news of the groom's arrival in the bridal suite, Priti had posed and laughed, offering wide, spontaneous smiles for the photographer who was snapping a series of portraits. Observing her, it was clear that the days when Indian brides were instructed to look demure and solemn for photographs commemorating this life-changing occasion were long gone.

Priti's mum had helped finalize plans for the wedding. She had collected ideas for various aspects of the event by taking photos of Indian television serials with her iPad and browsing the Internet for inspiration. She had visited websites like maharaniweddings.com, a blog designed for 'the day-dreaming Indian bride searching for her unique wedding style' to look for unique ideas, and a website that fills a digital gap in the wedding industry by providing easy access to visual online content for brides living outside India who are keen on finding ideas, inspiration and vendors online for distinctly Indian weddings. The beauty of maharaniweddings.com is that the photographs on display are all of real weddings that have, mostly, taken place in the US.

The website maintains that 'readers trek the globe looking for wedding ideas that are reflective of their cultural heritage'. And this is true. Many brides still choose to travel to India to shop for their wedding clothes and accessories. Stores in India cater to the influx of shoppers from abroad during the cooler winter months which coincide with half-term dates when families abroad have more leisure to travel.

But travelling down to India to shop for their wedding is not an option open to all prospective brides living abroad. The reality is that most of these young women are working professionals who must save their annual leave for their wedding and honeymoon. Understandably, they need to find their wedding finery closer home.

This was the case with Priti as well. After much consideration, her family had decided not to travel to India to shop for her trousseau.

'For us, it was finances, family and the inconvenience of travelling to India,' she would tell me later.

The UK-based Asian wedding industry has, in fact, taken note of those prospective brides who can't travel to India to shop for their wedding paraphernalia. Throughout the year, you can find 'Asian wedding expos' being held across the country. These range from high-end shows organized by the likes of Aashni & Co, which present designers like Manish Malhotra and Varun Bahl to UK audiences, to *Asiana Wedding* exhibitions in London and Birmingham. Like other similar events, these exhibitions offer prospective brides and their families a taste of the latest trends in Asian fashions, foods, flower arrangements, make-up, decoration ideas and so on. The atmosphere at such events is buzzing and some brides are likely to come away from them feeling more confused than ever by all the pricey options at their disposal.

'If I could do it again, I'd go to India,' Priti now admits. 'I think, more than anything, it's a memory that you went shopping for your wedding with your family in India which makes it so special.'

But what do you really need to make a wedding distinctively Indian? Is it the fashion and the decorations that make it Indian or the religious ceremony which constitutes an integral part of it?

From the many conversations I had with brides who live around the world and have an Indian-style wedding, I learn that their decisions were overwhelmingly driven by the fact that they felt familiar with and emotionally closer to both the visual and spiritual aspects of a typically Indian wedding. It's what they were used to seeing and experiencing as guests at other Indian weddings, and the ceremonies and traditions they witnessed symbolized marriage to them as nothing else could, even though they had been born and raised outside India.

I remember walking into the ceremony hall at Priti's wedding and being awed by the elaborate decorations put up everywhere. The room dripped with pink and red crystals and the wedding altar, where the bride and groom would observe the marriage rituals, glimmered in the light. Flower petals arranged in rows led to huge Ganesha statues sitting on either side of the aisle down which Priti would walk to the altar.

Everyone was requested to take their seats. We were told to hush as the ceremony began. But before it did, the pandit introduced himself to us. He addressed us in Hindi and then translated his words into English. He described his role in the ceremony, explaining that he was not there simply to preside over the ceremony, but also to explain to us the meaning of the ancient Sanskrit vows the bridal pair would make to each other. Marriage, he went on, was considered one of the most important of the *samskara*s or life cycles in the Hindu tradition; it celebrated the union of two families and two people in a sacred bond. It was important that we focus on the ceremony, he said, because we had a lifelong role to play as witnesses to the promises exchanged by the couple.

The ceremony began with the pandit leading a prayer to bless the groom and his family. It was then that Priti made her grand entrance. We all turned to gaze at her. Flanked by her brother and male cousins, she was ushered into the ceremony hall under a canopy of flowers. A romantic Bollywood melody chosen by her played softly in the background.

A white cloth was unfolded and held up lengthwise in front of the groom so that he was hidden from Priti's view. He would be revealed to her once she walked up to the altar. Years ago, when the dictates of family elders prevailed, many couples were not even given the opportunity of meeting each other before the wedding ceremony, and a moment such as this one usually served as the occasion on which the prospective bride and groom first laid eyes on each other. I think about my husband's maternal grandmother, now in her eighties, who once told me about her wedding. 'I had no idea who I was getting married to, I had never met him, or even seen a photograph of him before our wedding.' She went on to say, 'The morning of our wedding I simply washed my hair and showed up for my lavan. I didn't wear any makeup and my hair was tied back. I wore a sari – in those days all brides wore saris. I don't think any photos were taken at the wedding. There weren't too many guests, just a few from my family and a few from his family. We served chai and snacks, got married and that was it, wedding over,' she had said. For Anil and Priti, who had met before and fallen in love, it was the first time in the day that they were seeing each other.

As the ceremony continued, the pandit shared a story with the guests.

'Who here [among those present here] knows how rice is grown?' he asked us all.

A few hands shot up.

'So then you know that rice seeds are first planted in a field, until the rice plant grows to about this height,' he went on, indicating a point located just below his knee. 'When the rice plant grows and reaches this level, it's plucked out of the soil and replanted in a new field where it will grow further, blossom and produce rice.

'So like the rice plant which must move to a new field in

order to blossom, Priti's parents must let her move to a new family, where she will grow and raise her own family.'

While the pandit was busy with his narration, I felt my husband quietly reaching for my hand. As my mind went back to my parents, whom I had left behind in America when I married and moved to London, I tried to control my tears.

Later that evening, more than fifteen hours after we had arrived to attend the wedding, the reception began drawing to a close. The deejays announced that the song now being played would be the last one. We were all well aware that, despite his announcement, he would agree to play at least another couple of songs, but we began saying our good-byes to the friends gathered there.

We looked around for Priti and found her standing panic-stricken near the door. Her eyes were bewildered and her smile had faded. She looked as if she were struggling to hold back tears and, on seeing us, reached over spontaneously to hug us. It was apparent that she wasn't ready for the wedding to be over so soon. She wasn't ready for the lights to go on, as it were, because that would signal that it was time for her, Anil's new wife, to make the move to Manchester.

When I meet Priti months after her wedding, she smiles and recalls the thoughts she had been entertaining at that particular moment.

'I got that "gulp" feeling,' she now confesses. That was when the reality of her new life had set in. 'I felt like I was being ripped apart, like I was suddenly no longer a part of my parents' family,' she goes on. 'My home would now be hundreds of miles away.'

She hadn't had time to pause and ponder over her situation; straight after the reception, she and Anil had made the journey up to the home they would share in Manchester.

In a culture that is so defined by relationships, a wedding is a time to celebrate family, heritage and customs, especially for those living outside India. For many large Indian families, the wedding serves as the new family reunion. Everyone must attend, because everyone, from the bride's maternal uncle to the groom's youngest cousin, has a role to play in the rituals. While Indian weddings are a celebration of sacred commitment, joining two lives and merging two families, they are also a time to reunite, bringing together again relatives scattered all over the world. Through the framework of an Indian wedding taking place outside India, that connection is underscored and intensified and the family bonds heightened, for a wedding of one culture will, most likely, follow a similar sequence of customs, whether it's held in Nairobi or Sydney, London or Toronto.

'When I look back at it, I know what my favourite part of the whole wedding was,' Priti says today. 'Early morning on my wedding day, I walked down the stairs of my house and my entire family was in a room together. They were waiting

151

to start the *chura* ceremony. Everyone was there: family from around the world, family that aren't on good terms with each other – everyone. That moment might not happen again, and the memory of seeing them all together for that one morning makes me smile.'

Selina shares the same feelings about her own wedding. She looks back fondly and acknowledges the benefits of having a destination wedding.

'By my getting married abroad, it allowed for both sides – the bride's side and groom's side – to really spend time with each other, to get to know each other. And that's what it's all about, isn't it? Joining us and joining our two families together.' She pauses for a moment, then adds, 'I had my dream wedding and I married my dream man.'

Alaska, USA

A JOURNEY INWARD

We land in Alaska with little more than a dinner invitation from a man I've never met.

Of all the destinations I've visited, I feel most unprepared as I arrive in Alaska, the daunting 'Last Frontier', as it were. From the moment we step out of the airport, the location itself, as marked on the globe, makes me feel distant from the world I know, as though by making the journey, I have stepped into another unfamiliar dimension.

For most people, the appeal of Alaska lies in its wild beauty. When you close your eyes and think of the state, the first images that come to mind are of its extraordinary national parks, fjords and snow-capped mountains and particularly, of its wildlife, 'Alaska's big five' – bears, wolves, caribou, dall sheep and moose – not to mention the whales, eagles and salmon that can be spotted by even the most amateur onlooker. These are Alaska's main attractions, according to most visitors.

But I am not among them.

I had decided to make the trip to Alaska after coming to

learn that a mandir, located in the city of Anchorage, was the northernmost temple in the world dedicated to the Hindu deity Ganesha. If there was a mandir, there had to be devotees, I surmised. As I began researching the subject, trying to find out more about the person who had built this mandir and about the people it was meant to serve, a clearer picture of the small Indian community living in America's northernmost outpost began to emerge.

At the Anchorage airport, my husband and I load up our grey Hyundai rental car. Though we're staying at a local bed and breakfast (B & B), over the next few days, this car will be like a second home for us as we drive hundreds of miles in and around the Anchorage area.

As we leave the airport, my fatigue bears down on me; my eyes have trouble focussing. The nearly 20-hour journey to Alaska from our last destination, Abu Dhabi – quite possibly, the opposite extreme in appearance and character to our current location – has taken its toll on my reserves of energy. Gone are the dusty roads, the crowded shopping areas, the searing-hot winds. We are surrounded, instead, by green needle trees, mountains on all sides and vast, peopleless streets.

I'm wound up tight and my mind is entangled in worries. We've recently packed up our last home and after weeks of travelling, we will need to find new jobs and a new home. There was a time when I loved the freedom of travel, but lately, I have an overwhelming need to feel anchored, to find a home and put down roots. I wish I could just allow myself to relax.

We should rest, but we don't want to waste our first few hours in Alaska. We pass stores like Wild West Guns and head downtown, where the quiet streets are lined with souvenir shops and furriers.

The Indian community here is small, unlike London's thriving one or even Dubai's, and numbers around 1,200, according to the 2010 census – a figure that is certainly higher than that of a state like Wyoming which has 500 Indians living within its borders, but is far lower than that of other American states like California, which has an Indian population of half a million, or New Jersey, which is home to a quarter million immigrants from India.

I had spoken over the phone to Sanjay Talwar, businessman and member of the Asian Alaskan Cultural Center, when I first began making plans to visit Alaska. Sanjay is not associated with the temple, but is a social anchor in the local community.

It's not all igloos and dog sleds up here, he had pointed out during our phone conversation, reminding me that 'we live *near* the mountains, not *on* the mountains'. I was curious to see this for myself. He had generously offered to host a dinner party for us when we were in town and promised to introduce us to the Indians in the community. 'I know everyone here. I'm like the Amitabh Bachchan of Alaska,' he'd declared with a roaring laugh.

When the Big B of Alaska invites you to his house, you don't turn him down. For me, his personality symbolized Alaska – generous, natural and larger than life.

Having made the long journey, we're now looking forward to meeting Sanjay at his home in a few days. Until then, we plan to venture out and explore our surroundings. Far from India, far even from the rest of America, I can already feel a sense of solitude and disconnect here. It's not so difficult to imagine Alaska's isolation from the rest of the country when you consider that Anchorage is the only American city to have 500,000 acres of state park at its border. In fact, Alaska has the largest state park overall, covering as much land as the state of Connecticut in terms of acreage alone. Locals refer to the rest of the United States as the 'lower 48' and proudly assert that Alaskans are kind and patient, unlike the indifferent and impatient people of the mainland states. Here in Alaska, there is pride in being the 'other' and as I interact with its people, I can feel and appreciate their distinctive identity and sense their individuality.

The older couple staying at our B & B chat with us as we sip coffee early the next morning at the breakfast table.

'You can't be too careful when it comes to bears. Just last week, a man got chomped.'

The woman says this casually, pouring local Alaskan birch syrup onto her pancakes. The syrup was made from trees growing nearby; it is dark and watery, but sweet. She helps herself to fresh fruit.

'Chomped?'

'Oh yes, by a bear,' she explains. 'And just down the road,' she points to a spot visible through the window, 'a man was kicked to death by a moose.'

The couple continues eating, as if these stories are mundane incidents and of little importance.

Mouths agape, my husband and I exchange wide-eyed glances; we've come to Alaska with plans to explore and enjoy the wilderness... The only problem is that it's April, too early for guided tours of the parks or cruises around the fjords, and too dangerous to go hiking off the designated path on our own. Guided tours of parks like the famed Denali National Park, which boasts over 9,000 square miles of parkland and preserve – making it larger than the American state of Massachusetts – begin in mid-May when the climate and cycle of life stabilize. Right now, the bears are waking up from their winter hibernation and they are hungry. Moose are overly protective of their newborn calves. Springtime in Alaska can be dangerous for the uninitiated. All around you is a reminder that this truly is wilderness, the habitat of animals which are wild.

The couple dispense advice over bites of breakfast. The man looks at us and outlines it in clear terms.

'Look,' he says, 'black bears – they want to eat you. Shoot them on sight. Grizzlies, well, they want to protect their turf. So just play dead if they appear in your path.'

I wasn't confident that I could tell the difference, in the heat of the moment, between a grizzly and a black bear; and

I certainly didn't plan to carry a gun. I was relieved when my husband agreed to do a more conservative sightseeing tour without stepping out of the safety of our little car.

We finish breakfast, end our conversation with the couple and head out.

To understand life in Alaska, you must first become acquainted with its grand landscape. We set off from Anchorage to drive down the Seward Highway, considered one of America's fifteen 'all-American roads', and among *National Geographic*'s 'drives of a lifetime'. The journey from Anchorage to the small seaside town of Seward, home to hardly 3,000, can be completed in a couple hours, but we stretch it out over a day. We stop off at places like Potter's Marsh, with its vantage points for bird-watching. We see mountains that rise sharply from the shoreline to heights of 4,000 feet and glaciers that feed streams. Waterfalls have become ice falls, frozen midway in their downward plunge. As we take in the spectacular views all around us, I wonder how much we can trust the face of nature, as it presents itself here, and the wilderness beyond.

We stop at Beluga Point, where hundreds of whales pass all through the summer months; about 400 beluga or white whales are to be found in the inlet alone. We hope for the chance to spot a beluga whale in the water, aware that this isn't the right season. But the landscape is so overwhelming that it impels us to put a halt to everything and try being a part of the scene, even if it's for a single moment.

We drive through Moose's Pass, where the town has a school for its forty children and a deli that is offering a special today – reindeer sausage burritos. A sign here says, 'Land of the midnight sun', and I'm reminded that in the northern tips of Alaska, the sun neither sets in the summer months, nor rises in winter. We travel through the Kenai Peninsula, where we stop by the emerald-green Kenai Lake and breathe in the fresh air.

We drive through avalanche-prone areas where horrifying natural disasters have taken place in recent history, a reminder that life in Alaska is always precarious, always one of extremes.

In the presence of such natural grandeur, I have no inclination to click photos and trivialize it. I can't imagine reducing all that I see before me to an insignificant image that can be edited, swiped or deleted whenever the mood strikes me. All I want is to breathe it all in and live with the memory.

Sanjay is already waiting for us when our car sweeps into his driveway and pulls up before the entrance. His house sits in a neighbourhood of manicured gardens, with a panorama of ice blue mountains serving as a distant backdrop.

His wife, Molina, warmly welcomes us into their home and leads us into a living room with tall windows and a view of the mountains. In the few minutes I have to speak to her alone, I learn that she is originally from Chandigarh and that before marrying Sanjay, she had never been anywhere beyond India's borders; in fact, she had applied for a passport only so that she could move with her husband to Alaska after her wedding.

As their friends begin trickling into the house, everyone is informal and there is a sense of familiarity as they regularly get together at each other's homes.

'We don't have our own families here in Alaska, so we've all become like an extended family,' says Aarti, one of the Talwars' younger guests who was born in India, but grew up mostly in Alaska.

Sanjay is an entertaining host and offers everyone red and white wine or – for the more daring – vodka cocktails. As everyone settles in, the room is abuzz with loud small talk in Hindi and English about the weather, recipes for homemade jalebis and the latest episode of the Kapil Sharma show on Indian television channels. We eat pakoras and guacamole and later in the evening, Sanjay and his friend, Anil, make fresh tandoori rotis on the barbecue grill outside to accompany the dishes that have been prepared for dinner.

The guests – close friends – are from all over India. There are couples from Bihar, Gujarat, Rajasthan and Punjab. The ladies are wearing a mix of suits, saris and tunics with leggings.

'I love how our Indian cultures mix here. You won't find that in the "lower 48",' says Aarti.

Although this isn't strictly true, the smaller population of Indians in Alaska, in comparison to that in other American states, does ensure a more intimate, cohesive group of people for whom their regional identities do not stand in the way of their unity or social interactions.

As I begin working my way around the room, chatting with each of the guests, I get to hear their stories and learn that for them, life in Alaska is isolated but comfortable, and Anchorage makes for a good home.

Oil firms, construction companies and, more recently, IT companies apparently bring most Indian nationals out to Alaska. There are many 'transitional Indians' who arrive here, explains Aarti. They come through companies like Wipro and Infosys and take up top IT jobs, typically staying for a year or so, before leaving. But the money is good here and with government initiatives like the Permanent Fund, whereby the state government provides residents a federal compensation every year to live in the state, the financial incentive to stay on is strong. For Sanjay and others, however, it's the lifestyle and more relaxed pace that keep them here.

'I came to Alaska because of my parents,' Sanjay tells me. 'Dad got a job with a petroleum company here. First, my dad came, then Mom and my older brother and later, me. In order for Dad to save enough money to buy all our airline tickets, he had to break up the expenses and bring us over one by one, over a period of three years.'

In India, Sanjay had lived in a big house, as a member of

an extended family living together under one roof, with his grandparents, uncles and cousins. His impression of America had been a distant one, formed by watching Hollywood movies and looking at photographs of the country taken when his uncle or other relatives visited it.

Sanjay was a young teenager when he arrived in Alaska and faced immediate culture shock.

'Our English wasn't very good compared to [that spoken by] Americans. There was a lot of American slang that I didn't know about. And actually, English was spoken better in those days. Nowadays, people can't speak a whole sentence without words like, "chill" or "yeah".'

Listening to Sanjay speak now, you can't tell that he once struggled to sound like a local. Throughout the evening, he offers us all the different reasons that make him love Anchorage the way he does – the lack of traffic congestion in the area, the good friends he's made, the business he's built and the outdoor life he has learned to enjoy.

While he's telling me about the wide range of outdoor activities residents can engage in, Sanjay suddenly runs down to the basement and hauls his camping and fishing gear up the stairs for me to take a look at.

'I enjoy fishing, camping and taking a car or motorhome out. My friend is a dentist and has a 55-foot boat. We go out fishing every weekend in the summer. And yes, it stays light out longer in the summer. In June, I played golf at 11.30 at night in daylight.'

The others laugh as Sanjay puts on his hiking and fishing gear in the living room. It's not as if they're all the outdoorsy type; some of them describe a trip when five or six families drove out to a scenic picnic spot, fried pakoras in the great outdoors and packed up to come back home. That was as close to camping as they cared to be.

Sanjay's mother, who is also at the dinner party, laughs and rolls her eyes as her son models his gear for us. I read the expression on her face – the universal one of a disapproving mother. *What a waste of money*, is clearly the thought that's running through her mind.

I sit with her for some time and listen to her account of the time she first arrived in Alaska over three decades ago.

'At that time, it was seven rupees to a dollar,' she begins.

Her early days in Alaska were difficult and weighed down by extreme loneliness. 'Earlier there were only two other Indian families here. Everyone felt such *akelapan* [loneliness],' she says.

I can tell that another guest, Kalpana or '*Behen* Aunty', as they affectionately refer to her, hasn't been able to shake off this feeling of isolation even years after living here. She later informs me that she is the only Gujarati in Alaska, as far as she knows, and that she came all the way here to be with her husband, but has stayed on for her two sons who like living here.

'They were born here, they have friends here, they like the open spaces,' she explains.

Kalpana comes from an extended-family household in

Gujarat. For her, during those first homesick years in Anchorage, it was 'all snow, and no family'. With her husband at work, she would spend her time at the local YMCA in order to learn English and while away the hours.

'There are still no Indian stores here,' she observes. 'But at least, now we have something to connect us back to India. Before, we had nothing, but now, we all have Indian channels. Do you watch *Comedy Nights with Kapil Sharma*?'

I don't, but I know my parents, who live in the "lower 48", don't miss a single episode.

Kalpana is an active member of the local community now and much loved by this group of friends. She has come to like life in Alaska.

'Life is too short,' she says. 'You have to enjoy it wherever you are.'

Coming back into the conversation, Sanjay's mother continues with her story.

'When we first arrived, I kept saying that I was going back. My husband would say, "Let's go shopping," but I didn't want to buy anything for the house. I didn't want to set up the house or stay here for long.'

Even Sanjay's father had planned to return to India.

'Everyone always says they'll make money, save money and retire in India. I've never seen this happen. You get old, you get sick and you get scared to go back to India,' Sanjay remarks. 'People just don't go back.'

'Now there are almost 25 [Indian] families here and I even

have seven grandchildren,' his mother volunteers. 'Now we are all permanent.'

After hours of enjoying generous hospitality and lively conversation about leaving India for Alaska and raising children here, where they have little exposure to Indian culture, as compared to other pockets in the country with a higher Indian population, we thank our hosts and leave for the night. They invite us to join them at the temple early on Sunday morning and we agree to see them there.

We have another day to explore the place before meeting our new friends at the temple. Our mornings are for driving and taking in the surroundings and after a few days in Alaska, I begin to feel more at home in this still unfamiliar environment.

Much as I admire nature, I fear it and respect its power. My husband pushes to drive further, to turn off the highway and explore solitary roads, to get out of the car and inch his way to the very edge of cliffs. It's not enough for him to see the sparkling water of the many creeks we pass; he must stop to dip his hands in and splash the water around. At every such halt along the way, he walks into the distance, throws his arms out and stretches, spontaneous and without inhibition, absorbing his new world in long, deep breaths. I prefer to remain in the car, writing notes. But his childlike wonder at the waterfalls, the trees and the vast open sky that surround us is enviable. I wish I, too, could forget the threat of bear attacks long enough to enjoy the moment as he is doing.

We continue our drive and as the road climbs, I begin to lose my bearings. Are the clouds hanging low or are we at a higher elevation? If we reach up, can we actually touch them and breathe in the air they are breathing?

Surrounded by a panorama of snowy peaks and glacial waters, the city girl in me senses why spiritual seekers find divinity in the mountains. The connection between mountainscapes and inner contemplation has been well documented for centuries in both Eastern and Western traditions. For so many, the journey inwards begins during a journey into the mountains.

Standing here at the foot of these ancient peaks is to stand in humble reverence. Their steady, rugged presence fills me with stillness and silence. I feel safe, cocooned in the valley between these towering guardians that connect the earth to the sky. I repeatedly scan the view, urging my eyes to capture every detail of this scene, but my eyes fail to adjust to the sheer scale of such natural splendour.

I cannot tell if I feel the presence of something higher than myself, as many often claim they do. But I do feel a momentary loss of self. I, too, am mountain, lake, cloud. For an instant, I let the pristine wind disengage me from my past and future, stripping me free of doubts and fears. I experience a sense of relief. Later, as the tears come, I feel renewed.

We head back to our B & B with an even greater appreciation of the awe-inspiring Alaskan landscape and a new awareness of how nature can soothe the spirit. It is nearly 10 p.m. and the April sky is still bright as we drive back down on Northern Lights Boulevard.

It's Sunday morning and a lone car is parked outside the Shri Ganesha Temple in Anchorage. The only Hindu temple in the state, this is arguably the northernmost mandir in the world dedicated to Lord Ganesha and certainly the northernmost Hindu temple in the country.

It's Sanjay's friend Anil's turn this week to prepare the temple for the Sunday puja and he has arrived early to do the needful. The duties involved in the upkeep of the temple are shared among committed local families and the responsibility of opening the temple is rotated every week. Unless a special festival is on, the temple is usually open for only a few hours every Sunday for the weekly ritual of worship.

Inside, Anil slides open a glass door to reveal familiar idols. In the centre stands a three foot-tall Lord Ganesha carved from black granite, a donation from Sat Guru Shri Sivaya Subramuniyaswami of the Kauai Aadheenam in Hawaii. There is, in fact, a story that until the day it was delivered to its current address in Anchorage, there was no place for it anywhere. To Lord Ganesha's right sit white marble idols of Rama, Sita, Lakshmana and Hanuman. To the left is Durga.

The temple is immaculately clean and has a newly built feeling about it, though it's been open to the public for a few years now. It has been designed with an 'arctic entry', a room that serves to prevent the Alaskan cold from invading the warm space within. Laid out with a bright green carpet, adorned with bouquets of peach, orange and red flowers and vibrantly clothed *murtis*, the interiors of the mandir present an inviting contrast to the fading grey of winter outdoors.

Anil aligns the chairs neatly for the devotees, before giving us a brief history of the space. The temple is especially meaningful for him, as he had taken the initiative and an active part in getting it constructed. He had helped secure the property and had led the constructions and renovation. He had worked with an architect, ensuring that the Indian-styled arches they were keen on had been incorporated in the design. While the building was simple, they had wanted the structure to look like a mandir.

Unlike other Indians who had come and settled in Anchorage in their youth, Anil had arrived at the age of 42 with a family. Soon after, he claims he had a vision to build the temple. A few fronted the money for all. Then Anil's boss matched the donation. Hinduism relies on donations for the upkeep of its temples and on the weekly contribution of home-cooked meals for the *parshaad* distributed after the puja.

As we wait, families begin to arrive at the temple; there are those we hadn't met at the dinner party and others who already feel like friends. In this small community, everyone knows everyone else quite well, but occasionally, there is the new entrant.

In fact, just then, one such unknown face sweeps into the temple, shoulders thrown back, running his fingers through his thick black hair. 'Hi, I'm Raj,' he says, introducing himself to the others.

If Sanjay is the Amitabh Bachchan of Alaska, here is the young Shah Rukh Khan. Though he's lived in Alaska for months, it is his first time at the temple.

'I thought it was time to get back to my roots,' he explains.

Sitting down beside me, he begins to tell me about himself as we eat our *langar* meal on disposable white plates.

'I'm the start of a new generation,' Raj declares. 'I'm the oldest in my family; so there's lots of pressure. But my dad just taught us not to worry about expectations, to go and do what we wanted.

'I came to study in Montana at the age of eighteen.'

Raj had studied at the University of Montana, another state with wide open spaces to live and breathe in and grow at that pivotal age in everyone's life. From Montana, he had found a good paying job as an accountant in Alaska and made the move.

'You like your open spaces, don't you?' I ask.

'I'm from a city of around eight million – Kolkata. I like having my own space now.'

While his estimate of Kolkata's population is somewhat exaggerated (it's closer to five million), Raj describes the cramped living conditions in his city. Going back to his hometown after years in the great American West was a jolt for him.

'I didn't go back to India for seven years,' he confides, 'and I suffered a major culture shock when I returned there. I thought, is this really where I grew up?'

He speaks with a laid-back American accent and I can be forgiven for assuming from his effortless ways and casual style of conversation that he was born and raised by a beach in California.

When he first arrived in America, he quickly made friends with non-Indians to get up to speed with the culture and language. 'I was always friends with people who weren't like me,' he confesses. 'I kept a pocket diary for all the words I didn't know. Then I'd read about the words and learn the cultural references later.'

He shares with me his plans for the next few years. He hopes to 'just live and move around until I'm thirty. Then I'll settle down. Maybe.'

He offers tips on what we should do during our last days in Anchorage. A self-described 'outdoorsy person', he recommends a number of places we should check out.

'Hike Flat Top. That's a sweet trail.'

He recommends places where we can eat.

'Bear's Tooth, catch a movie and a beer.'

But above all, he recommends with a beaming smile, 'Live a little. Be daring.'

This seems to be the advice followed by anyone who moves to Alaska.

Since the Anchorage temple is so small, there is no official priest to conduct the services. The attendees often take turns to lead the prayers and today, Nishi performs the *aarti* and leads the prayers. Originally from Bihar, she has lived all over the world with her husband, an ex-Army man.

'Growing up in India, you attend all these pujas, but you don't know what it all means,' she says. 'But since I'd been teaching the kids at Sunday schools outside India, I had to learn, because the kids, they ask so many questions. "Why do we turn to the right and not to the left? Why do we recite this mantra and not that one?" I had to teach myself, so I could teach them.'

She laughingly admits how her mother and her family back in India were shocked to hear that she led the prayers and taught children.

'I had two years of Sanskrit in school. That came in handy when I was learning the mantras and the meanings. The rest, I've taught myself.'

From Cremona to London to Montreal and now Alaska, it is the children of the diaspora who spurn the need to reconnect and to pass on the culture of those who had originally left India. Unknowingly, a generation that had left India to live abroad would become ambassadors of an identity and keepers of tradition.

During the puja, Kalpana or '*Behen* Aunty', as I now think of her, blows the conch shell and includes my husband and me in the service. We take turns ringing a bell and scattering flower petals as prayers are recited. For a surreal moment, there we are, the two of us, leading a puja at the front of a mandir in Alaska. As the ceremony comes to an end, Nishi instructs us to spin around as a final mantra is read.

Speaking to her later, I ask why we needed to spin in place. She explains that this movement is meant to symbolize the belief that while we are engaged in performing these elaborate rituals, God resides in us.

Standing in that temple, I am inclined to agree with her. While I haven't forgotten Raj's quip – 'Live a little. Be daring.' – there is something about the ambience of this sacred space that, despite its external trappings, seems a natural extension of the feeling of cleansing and renewal Alaska's wilderness had evoked in me earlier. Having moved from one country to the next, from urban spaces to ones where nature reigns, I have come to accept that, no matter which corner of the world we live in; how we choose to pray or what kind of rituals we follow, ultimately, God lives within each one of us. And while the outward manifestations of culture and tradition are passed down from one generation to the next, our spirituality transcends geographical distances from one end of the world to the other, brooking neither borders nor thresholds, borne along by individuals who are connected to memories of a home within.

Florida, USA

AGEING ABROAD

We scatter her ashes over the side of a hired boat.

Thousands of miles from where she began her life, Naurati Devi returns to earth and drifts into the Thames. I fear I will, one day, join her in this river and I am overcome by the urge to go home.

When packing up and moving abroad, the obvious consideration driving our decision is where and how we will be living. Many of us forget, however, that choosing a new home abroad may also determine our final resting place.

The thought hadn't occurred to me earlier, but when I find myself attending a series of funerals mourning the passing of elders in my husband's family, I am forced to confront it. It seems to be the season of death and the local temples and funeral homes are overbooked. We spend a few weeks witnessing the last rites of the deceased and joining in prayers. We attend funerals for distant relatives that even my husband can hardly remember. But others are closer to home, like his grandmother, Nauratri Devi, who had been known as 'Maa Ji' both within the family and in the wider local community. A proud woman who had raised four children across India, East Africa and England, she had ensured that her indomitable will prevailed till the end.

I fondly remember the first time I met her as a new bride and a recent addition to the family. With furrowed brow and a hint of sternness, she had asked me why I wasn't wearing a bindi or red lipstick – I was a new bride, after all, wasn't I? Actually, I hadn't even considered it when getting ready to visit her at the nursing home for patients suffering from dementia. She had laughed, embraced me warmly and soon forgotten who I was and why I was visiting her.

It is evident that Maa Ji was well-respected in the community. Marquees fill up with guests for the pujas and *havans* that follow her passing. It strikes me that her life had been lived across continents and touched many people, some of whom had shared her journey from India and Africa to London. Like Maa Ji's life, mine too has been lived across borders, divided between two countries, with my family and friends based both in America and in the UK. Among the ones living in England, most know me as my husband's spouse, an identity that represents only one aspect of my life. Will my early years as a single woman be recollected at all, I wonder, if I pass away while living in the UK? Will my ashes end up in London, like Maa Ji's, or be sent back to where I was born? I have friends who were obliged to fulfil the unfortunate duty of carrying their loved ones' ashes from America to India to perform their last rites. It is one thing to live abroad, but another to die on foreign shores.

Of course, all these thoughts are trivial, as my husband reminds me. 'Does it really matter?' he asks. 'Will you really care, you know, when you're dead?'

Besides, I should have thought about all this before moving abroad. But I hadn't.

Having left my home in America for adventures abroad, I've ended up like so many of the people I've interviewed for this book – caught between two lives, the before and the after. I've lived in the UK long enough to have created a home, a career and a busy life that keeps me tied to a place that once enchanted me. But still, I wake up every morning and wonder when I'll return 'home', to the place where I grew up and where my family still lives. That was always the plan, after all – to live abroad for a few years, then pack up and return home, triumphant and enriched by my time abroad and, deservedly, smug about having lived outside the confines of my small hometown.

Yet, as with so many others, my life abroad has been extended indefinitely; one year became two, then three; and now it's my eighth year in the UK. I've lived here long enough to feel like a tourist when I'm back home, visiting unfamiliar places that have been built over my memories from childhood and my early twenties. But curiously enough, I can't shake off the feeling that the UK isn't really my home either. Living between two worlds can make anyone feel liberated, on the one hand, and a misfit, on the other, with homes and relationships in both places, while not fully belonging to either.

Time moves swiftly and the thought of growing old and dying in another country makes me unreasonably anxious. Similarly, the thought of something happening to my family, especially my parents, while I'm away is equally unbearable.

It's the one burden I have carried within me all these years after moving out of the country of my birth – the guilt of leaving my parents behind, a guilt inherited, perhaps, from them, for they too had left their parents behind in India to begin a new life in another land. Life can be so painfully absurd: we are raised with love and care, only to move away from the very people who have nurtured us in order to follow our own individual paths. Mine led me to London, but despite or, perhaps, because of the distance that separates me from my parents, I remain preoccupied with thoughts of them living alone as age and its infirmities creep up on them. I worry about how, living so far away, I will take care of them when they really need me. As they grow old in America, far from northern India where they had been born and brought up, I wonder if they too are brooding over the same concerns that take hold of me. I wonder if they are content with their present situation and how and where, given a choice, they would wish to spend the remaining years of their lives. Would they want to return to India or is America truly home?

Such thoughts are hardly unique to my situation, I realize, and soon, I find myself searching for stories of Indians growing old abroad. And the search leads me to Florida.

When we arrive in Orlando, the weather is muggy. The July heat is soaring past 32 degrees Celsius. It's my first visit to this place and I have reservations about its appeal. In my mind, I imagine that it is a city for the very young, who are drawn to the attractions of Disney, or for the very old, who have come to Florida following retirement.

In Orlando, a city that is regularly voted the most visited place in America, we find ourselves surrounded by an infinite number of restaurants, shopping malls and places to go to for entertainment. Contemplating the attractions of this destination that is such a hot favourite with tourists, I wonder what it might be like for those who actually live here.

The purpose of our trip is to visit family. Before hitting the theme parks and attractions, we spend a day driving down streets lined with palm trees and visiting the homes of relatives. I keep an eye out for alligators, wary that they might spring a nasty surprise, unlikely as it is for us to encounter one on the streets. We do make a quick stop later at Gator Golf and Adventure Land, where we see alligators soaking in the waters around a miniature golf course.

The families we're visiting settled in Florida decades ago, having lived in India, East Africa and the UK before moving to America. At one of the homes we visit, an aunt and her husband lead us on a tour of the enormous back garden where they spend hours tending to the tropical fruits and vegetables they are growing. From mangoes to guavas to avocados, they grow them all. They're especially proud of their herb garden, where they nurture plants like neem, tulsi (basil) and others which, they say, are useful and effective in Indian medicinal treatments.

'Smell this lemongrass,' Aunty suggests, eagerly waving it in front of me so that I can take a sniff.

'We mix all of these together and make green smoothies every day,' she adds, flashing us her trademark wide smile.

It is a delight walking through the lush garden and observing how their interest in it enlivens and animates them. I even consider the joy it might give my parents if they were to move to warm and sunny Florida and pick up gardening as a hobby.

We visit another family which lives just a few minutes' drive away. From the outside, their house looks no different from many others in Florida, but its interiors are inspired by the havelis of Rajasthan. Wherever you look, you will notice features that were designed especially for this home. Arranged throughout the first floor of the house are lanterns waiting to be lit at Diwali; peacock patterns run along the pelmets from which draperies hang and heavy carved wooden doors open into other rooms. The whole house feels like a living, breathing piece of artwork and the creative force behind this is a lady named Gauri or 'Aunty', as we call her.

The beauty of the house lies in the details and in her personal touches. It was she who had sketched the peacock designs that became the moulds for the metal staircases; and it was she who hand-sewed the intricate patterns that frame the curtains.

Art and, especially, sewing are dear to Gauri's heart. Through conversations we've had earlier, I've come to know about the 'Orlando Sewcial', an initiative that she's a part of. This is a group that she, along with two other Indian American women, Kumud and Madhu, helped set up to bring people from the local community together around the shared hobby of sewing. What started off as an idea discussed by the women during a Ramayana study group has blossomed into an organization that attracts around 20 to 25 women to sewing-related social events throughout the year. While the group is open to everyone, including members of the Florida Sewing Sew-ciety, it often draws women, especially older ones, from the local Indian community.

'It's really the older women who drive this,' Gauri says. In fact, many of the most committed members of this women's group are over 65.

The group gets together regularly to work on sewing projects, producing a wide range of garments, accessories and household goods, from caps and jackets to pillowcases, which are then donated to local charities, hospitals and shelters for the homeless.

While the pieces they tailor help the local community, sewing together is an activity that has helped some of the women in the group find a meaningful space for themselves where their contributions count, and where they can interact socially with others. This is especially true for those members of the older generation who may have spent most of their lives in India, before being brought over to America by their children who had moved abroad earlier. For such individuals across America, the transition can be difficult and painful. For some, the language barrier hinders social interactions. For others, lack of transportation limits their engagement in social activities that require them to step out of the house.

Gauri tells me about one member of the group, an 80-year-old wheelchair-bound woman who can only communicate in Hindi.

'Her son brings her to the group. She is one person who has really touched my heart. She shows up every week; she tells us it's the one thing that she looks forward to every week.'

In spite of living in a home surrounded by family, life in America can be an extremely lonely experience for the aged. With their busy work schedules, the adult members may have little time to spare for them, while the children, away at school for much of the day, are tied up in their leisure time with after-school and weekend activities. While the different generations may be happy living together, the oldest members of the family can find themselves left to their own devices for the greater part of the day. Unable to keep pace with the demanding schedules of the younger generation and lacking the ability to go out and forge social bonds on their own, they find themselves increasingly isolated.

Orlando Sewcial is a boon for elderly women caught in a

similar situation. Set up with the purpose of bringing people together through a creative outlet, this initiative allows them to share in 'the joy of learning something new and being productive,' as Gauri puts it. 'It gives the women in the group a chance to meet new people, get involved, enjoy the camaraderie,' she adds. 'I've noticed that in the group, people have started a "buddy system", where they go shopping for fabrics together and help each other with learning sewing techniques. They like the charity concept also, giving back to the community.

'Sewing is a great way to keep our brains engaged,' she goes on. 'Sewing, knitting – it all requires a lot of mathematics. Reading and figuring out patterns, calculating measurements, estimating fabric, it's highly beneficial to keep the mind active while being creative.'

Gauri hopes that it is of special benefit to the older women in the community who might not be as active as they once were due to their age and the circumstances of living on the peripheries of a busy household.

'So many of the women say that they used to sew or embroider back in India. They were taught by their mothers when they were young, but they haven't had the need to sew while in America.'

By engaging older women socially and mentally, Gauri feels that Sewcial can help them combat their ennui and sense of isolation and make them feel empowered and useful to the local community.

For many, retiring to the 'sunshine state' of Florida is the last chapter of the American dream. With consistently pleasant weather all the year round and palm trees everywhere that make you feel like you're on permanent vacation, it's easy to understand why so many Americans look forward to retiring down south. It's no surprise, then, that in the last few years, retirement homes catering to the needs of the country's growing elderly Indian population are beginning to pop up in Florida.

As an entire generation of Indian immigrants in America is beginning to age, they constitute the fastest growing group of seniors in major cities across states like New York and Texas, where the Indian population is considerable. A 2015 study undertaken for the American Association of Retired People (AARP) on the South Asian community in Houston and beyond indicates that there is a clear need for senior citizen-related services geared to address the preferences of this growing group through language, cuisine and understanding of traditions.

A quick Google search reveals that the market is responding to this new and growing breed. Around the country, organizations like India Home in New York have started to address issues faced by local seniors in the South Asian community, and retirement communities for Indians are springing up on both the East and West Coasts.

ShantiNiketan, in central Florida, became the first retirement community in the country to specifically cater to American citizens of Indian origin. With a community prayer room, Indian meals and provisions for cultural activities, it tapped into a new market that has been growing over time and will be booming in the coming years. Since ShantiNiketan opened, other retirement communities for Indians in America have come onto the scene. Priya Living in California, with its vibrant and modern aesthetic, invites its residents to 'leave the door open', 'play' and 'sip chai with neighbors'. In New Jersey, the chain of My Indian Nursing Home celebrates Indian festivals throughout the year with its residents.

While many seniors choose not to move out of the areas where they had settled, and have continued living for decades, some are looking to retire in areas that offer a more temperate climate, making Florida an ideal destination.

To find out more about such communities in Florida, I get in touch with Anand, sales director of Anand Vihar, one of the new Indian retirement communities currently being developed in Tampa. Despite the fact that it is still a work in progress at the time of our phone interview, clients are already buying and reserving plots in the community.

I had first learnt about Anand Vihar through an advertisement and was intrigued when I discovered that it was being built with retired people from the Indian community in mind. According to the advertisement, the planned gated community would include homes and condos for those over the age of 55 and would feature leisure amenities for the residents, including walking trails across its grounds and yoga and fitness classes, among others. The key feature of the community was the central club house, almost like a country club, where lunch and dinner would be prepared every day to suit the dietary requirements and palates of the Indian residents. Vegetarian dishes and Indian cuisine were to be a key selling point for the community.

While speaking to Anand about his project, I come to know just how much of a draw the pleasant climate is for prospective residents of the community. Many of their potential buyers are from the northeastern states of America. Some had emigrated earlier from India to East Coast hotspots like New York and New Jersey; others are from the major cities of the American Midwest, like Detroit or Chicago, that endure severe winters with freezing temperatures. Now that these buyers have reached a point in their lives where they can step away from their jobs, they are looking to retire in a place where the climate is warm and the ambience relaxed. But even more than the climate and amenities, what is attracting residents to this place, according to Anand, is a shared sense of community.

'They want to be around like-minded individuals and have like-minded conversations over lunch and dinner, sharing their life experiences about coming here [from India] and starting from scratch,' he explains.

Regardless of which part of America they come from, future residents already have much in common. Many of them arrived in America as immigrants in the 1960s and '70s and did well for themselves. Their careers earned them wealth and success and, having worked hard for decades, they are now ready for a life of relative ease in Florida.

The target market for the retirement community is clearly defined. It's geared for the newly retired active Indian immigrant who has lived and worked in the country for years, not for the much older generation who had, perhaps, moved to America in their old age to live with their adult children. Citing an example closer to home, Anand tells me about his 80-year-old grandmother who is living with his parents after coming over from India. For her and for others of her generation, moving to America to live with their offspring can, at times, feel like a prison sentence. Being confined indoors, unable to interact with anyone, while everyone else in the family is either at school or at work or busy with their daily routines, can be a lonely and alienating experience. The goal that retirement communities like Anand Vihar and others coming up across the country set themselves is to cater to a slightly younger generation, whose members have lived in the US for years. In their early sixties now, they are looking to lead active, independent lives.

For this generation, among the first to live and settle in the States, it's the beginning of a cultural shift, whereby choosing to live independently in your twilight years and not necessarily with your children in their homes is becoming the approved norm, rather than the frowned-upon exception.

'Early on, when the first generation moved to America, it was very taboo to consider putting your parents into assisted living. They lived with the son,' Anand goes on, filling me in on traditional mindsets and the attitudinal shift that has occurred, helping retirement communities like the one he is building to gain acceptance and approval. 'Now, as this first generation is approaching their sixties and seventies, they don't have that mindset. They don't want to live with their kids, because they still have robust, active daily, weekly schedules. They're like, "Look, you lived under my roof for all these years; I'm not going to turn around and live under your roof and live by your rules now. We still have our lives." It is no reflection on the kids; the parents are just still very independent and active.'

For Harish, 70 years old and a buyer, the lure of moving down south to Florida from his home in New Jersey was the warmer climate and the prospect of living near his daughter and grandchildren. His wife, especially, was enticed by the prospect of living closer to their grandchildren, he says. It just so happens that his son-in-law, Santosh, is the founder of Anand Vihar; so it was fitting that Harish would be among the first residents of the new community.

'Our house is being built and will be ready in January or February — only a few months away,' Harish tells me. 'It's a four-bedroom home with three bathrooms and a spacious living room.'

What enthuses him the most is the idea of being surrounded by retired people 'just like me' so that he can be assured of compatible company during the day and in the evening. They can play cards together, go out together in Tampa, he muses aloud.

After living in New Jersey for over four decades, however, it was difficult for Harish and his wife to arrive at the final decision to move.

Originally from Mumbai, Harish moved to New Jersey in the 1970s after completing his undergraduate studies in Detroit. He came to the East Coast to do his MBA in Connecticut, then went on to complete a Master's from the New Jersey Institute of Technology after getting married. Since his graduation from NJIT, he has remained in New Jersey, living near Clifton, north of Newark.

What drew him to New Jersey and encouraged him to go on living there was the robust local Indian community. In the 1970s, New York and New Jersey had large Indian populations and Harish enjoyed being a part of a wider Indian–American community. There were more Indians living there than in Detroit, where the ice-cold winds blowing in from the surrounding Great Lakes were too much for him to bear. Once they were comfortably settled in New Jersey, Harish and his wife decided it was time to start a family. They have four daughters, three of whom still live in the New York metropolitan area, while the fourth lives in Tampa.

'The decision to move was tough,' Harish remembers. 'I miss the people in New Jersey; we lived there for a long time. But eventually, we had to make a decision. It was getting too cold and we wanted to be close to one of our daughters.'

Florida's welcoming climate has, in fact, made a difference to their lives. While living in New Jersey, Harish and his wife had enjoyed an active social life for much of the year, but once the long winter set in, lasting for nearly four months, the freezing weather would confine Harish to the house, making him feel trapped. Now the couple can socialize all through the year.

'We've already met our new neighbours and have made friends,' he says contentedly.

After moving to Florida, Harish had reached out to the Indian Senior Citizens group in Tampa and become a member.

'There are 150 to 200 members,' he informs me. 'They meet twice a month – the first and third Wednesday of each month. We play cards and carom board and other games. We meet from eleven to three and around two, we have tea and cookies. They sometimes have singers come, who perform old Bollywood songs which we enjoy; and some days, they invite speakers to come and talk to us, giving [us] medical advice or financial advice about retirement.'

Moreover, since Tampa has a large Indian community – it was the first US city to host the International Indian Film Academy (IIFA) awards, I am told – there are cultural and religious activities available at the local temple for anyone who might be interested.

The social aspect of such a lifestyle is key to Harish's well-being and that of others like him who have reached a certain age. It's been three years since he retired from his job at IIT, where he had worked for more than thirty years. Since depression and anxiety among elders in the community are major issues brought on by physical and social isolation, engaging in social activity is key to maintaining sound physical and mental health. It's important for Harish and those in his situation to stay active in their retirement years, to have company and make friends.

As was the case with my parents, when Harish moved to the States, it had never occurred to him that he would end up spending the rest of his life there. He concedes, however, that he began enjoying his life in America and felt settled during the initial years following his move. He still visits India regularly and, over the last decade, has been returning there every year. At the same time, his brother who still lives in India visits the US frequently.

'The connection is still there. I don't feel disconnected from India,' Harish says. 'And since I am [living] in the Indian community here, I don't feel the lack of connection.'

Proud though he is of the initiative his daughter and son-in-law have taken in setting up Anand Vihar, he is aware that it's not a unique venture; such Indian communities are popping up in cities like Houston, Baltimore and anywhere where there are large populations of retiring Indians.

Other than the pleasant climate and the social activities on offer at retirement homes for the Indian community, another big draw for potential residents is the availability of Indian meals. At Anand Vihar, in particular, the on-site preparation of Indian meals is a key feature, Anand informs me.

'The cooking is a big thing,' he explains, 'and what is interesting is that, on a few occasions, the wife of a prospective resident has pulled me aside and said, "I'm worried about passing away before my husband. He doesn't even know how to work a microwave. I want to make sure that cooking [cooked Indian meals] is available for him." It is interesting to see how they are so unselfish. For some, the rationale for looking to live somewhere like this is to make sure their spouse is taken care of.'

Born in America to immigrant parents, Anand has an interesting perspective on the generations.

'With the first generation, most of their marriages were arranged, but I am surprised by how much love I actually see between the couples,' he observes. 'I now believe that it is absolutely true that love grows; you don't have to be in love at the beginning. A lot of the couples I meet have grown in love and I see them caring for each other. It is not the typical mentality [of couples moving here] to think that it is one person making the decision; it is a shared decision.'

Deciding where to settle after retirement and when to make the move isn't necessarily up to the couple alone. The desire or obligation to help raise grandchildren can often stand in the way of choosing to retire in Florida. Grandparents can, after all, be a coveted support for many young parents who need help with school drop-offs and pickups and would prefer family elders at home to keep an eye on the children, instead of hiring relative strangers as babysitters.

'A lot of the decision-making, it is shared with the family,' Anand informs me. 'A lot of them say, "I need to have a discussion with my kids." The kids could be scattered, living all over the country with one in California and one in New York and then the parent wants to move to Florida.

'I have seen some sad occasions, where potential buyers had to cancel their reservation,' he goes on, adding another dimension to the decision-making process. 'I felt really bad for them. They need help taking care of their children. Other times, the clients choose to defer their decision to move because they want to be with their grandkids.'

In so many ways, they are members of a generation that doesn't stop giving to the next.

'Tomorrow, I am meeting a couple,' Anand adds, 'and they're coming with their son. Kids want to make sure their parents are in an environment and a location they approve of so that they themselves feel comfortable having them living so far away from where they've grown up.'

Like many of the people I've interviewed for this book, potential residents of Anand Vihar have come to a decision that they will not be going back to India, even though their original plan may well have been to move to America, make a pile and return to their roots one day.

'A lot of these retirees would spend part of the year in India, like in the winter months, and then return to America during the summer, to be with their families and grandkids, etc.,' Anand elaborates. 'What I am finding now is that for a lot of them, the journey to India is very tiring. They'd rather just come down to Florida and enjoy it and maybe, do India every two or three years or maybe, every other year. Just that journey to

India and going through that whole process…as they get older, they don't want to make that journey anymore.'

He shares the reasons potential buyers often offer for staying on in America: 'We've been here long enough in the US, and now we've come to embrace Western culture and the luxuries of Western lifestyle.'

Though I don't get to explore the Tampa retirement community during my trip to Florida and discover for myself if it is, indeed, the ideal place for Indian immigrants in America to retire, as Anand makes it out to be, it is touching to hear the stories of a formidable generation that is reaching a new age, but looking to make an independent and comfortable space for itself. These are the men and women who had left India to build new lives in America through sheer determination and hard work, and I cannot help recall Gauri Aunty's remark in connection with the older women in the Orlando Sewcial group. 'In America, there is a different mindset when it comes to getting older, compared to that in India. People are still willing to try new things, to keep driving, to keep moving forward. They don't give up because they think they're too old. There's an independent spirit.'

Some of the stories unfolding around us of an ageing generation of immigrants from India bear her out. There is the couple from upstate New York who can no longer bear to live through yet another winter of blizzards and others who are tired of their relentless work schedules and crave more relaxed days in a more temperate climate. And how can one forget the recently widowed woman who is desperate to move to a retirement community to escape the oppressive solitude she is unaccustomed to? But there are other stories too. Consider the widowed grandfather who resists moving out of his home, fiercely struggling to maintain it in the pristine condition his late wife had left it, refusing to buy new furnishings to replace the pieces she had chosen, now weathered by time. I wonder about my own parents, still fit and active, who spend their evenings having dinner together, smiling in nostalgia as they listen to songs from old black-and-white Bollywood movies. What are their thoughts about the hundreds of miles separating them from their children? Would they ever consider the idea of moving from the place where they have made their lives and settling into a new environment like the residents of the growing retirement communities?

Anand captures the duality of their situation perfectly when he says, 'They can't see themselves going back to India, but they still want that culture. They want to keep that relation and camaraderie with fellow retirees, but they also want the luxuries that they are used to now in the US; so, they can't move back to India.'

Moving, ultimately, is about leaving one home for another, taking with you only the most essential of accumulated possessions, along your memories. However, where the idea of moving might once have seemed to the senior generation of

Indian Americans like an adventure into the exciting unknown, it is now driven by the quest for comfort, for the familiar, often tinted by the colours of nostalgia for a home from long ago.

Washington, DC

RETURNING HOME

Every afternoon, Lucky[1] returns from work and checks his mailbox. For years, he has been waiting to receive notice of the documents that will enable him to live and work in the US – legally. For too long now, he has been living under the radar.

On a humid summer's day in Washington, DC, I'm on my way to conduct one of the final interviews for this book. I will be meeting Lucky or 'Millionaire Lucky', as some of his friends call him, in acknowledgement of his ethos of working hard, maintaining a clean lifestyle and successfully saving his hard-earned money.

'He learned to speak English only after moving here,' his friend tells me. 'And guess what? Now he's fluent in Spanish too!'

Lucky owns and runs a popular food-truck business in the city that caters to breakfast and lunchtime customers. In the evening, he parks his truck outside the restaurant owned by his friend, whom he addresses as 'Bhaji'.

Moving beyond the Capitol Hill area, we drive further on into Southeast DC, one of the relatively unsafe areas of the capital city. I remember always worrying about my dad, a taxi driver in DC, knowing that he often ferried passengers to these very localities at night. But in broad daylight, the area seems innocuous. As we approach the restaurant, I notice that we are in the shadow of the Nationals Park, the ballpark where the Washington Nationals, DC's Major League Baseball team, hosts its games.

We pull up in front of the entrance. The food truck is already parked there and we wait for Lucky to appear. Minutes later, he comes out and greets us warmly, before climbing into the car where we will engage in a conversation over the next few hours. Lucky is tall and lean. Now that his workday is over, he has changed into a grey joggers and a T-shirt. A gentle smile lights up his face and his tone, as he speaks to us, is respectful.

My manner is hesitant, as I begin my interview in my trademark faltering Punjabi.

Lucky bursts into laughter. 'You can speak in English,' he says, encouraging me to switch to the language I am comfortable with.

Then with his eyes downcast, he begins to share his story with me.

When Lucky set out from his home in Punjab to seek his fortune overseas in May 1999, he had to leave his new bride behind.

'She was still wearing her *chura*,' he now murmurs.

At the time, she was pregnant with their only child. Their son would be born while Lucky was still making the journey to America without any legal papers, choosing a dangerous route to his final destination that would take him months to reach and finally enter. Aware that if he went through the proper channels and applied for a visa, his application would, in all likelihood, be turned down, the young man had decided that a chance to work in America was worth the risks involved and the sacrifices it entailed.

To meet the expenses of his son's journey to America, Lucky's father had sold off some of the family-owned land. The money from the proceeds would cover the fee charged by the agent who was making the travel arrangements for Lucky's trip to America, beginning with a flight from Delhi to Costa Rica.

That journey had been undertaken nearly two decades ago, but in the last few years, an increasing number of South Asians have been trying out the Latin American immigration route, taking advantage of a migrant trail into America that has existed for years. According to a news article published in 2016 in the *Los Angeles Times*, which cites US Customs and Border Protection statistics, more than 4,000 Bangladeshis, Indians, Nepalis and Pakistanis travelled to the US along a route originating in Brazil, compared with just 225 such migrants who had done so seven years earlier.[2] Most of those who chose to travel by this route were arrested while crossing into the US illegally.

What had motivated them to do so is not difficult to

understand when I listen to Lucky's own reasons for undertaking the journey.

'At the time, all I wanted was to come to America to work. It was a craze.'

He couldn't, however, have foreseen the horrors of the journey that lay ahead. From Costa Rica, he was taken to Nicaragua in an 18-wheeler truck, along with other aspirants like him. As they neared the border, they were made to get off the vehicle and walk the distance. This involved climbing up a steep hill and then sliding down.

'We all got injured, suffering bruises and cuts, but we made it and found each other again at the spot where we all spent the night,' Lucky now recalls. 'It was around two a.m. when we found each other. The next day, the agent took us again via the 18-wheeler across Nicaragua to Honduras, Guatemala and then Mexico.'

Once they had reached Mexico, the group travelled in the truck trailer for three days and two nights without a break. Before they boarded the vehicle for this particular leg of the journey, the agent had warned Lucky and the others that they wouldn't have anything to eat or drink for the next few days. There were over 300 people packed into the vehicle, with little space to move and the stench inside was sickening.

'There was no room to stretch your legs out; we were all crammed and stuck in there together,' Lucky tells me, the memory of the experience still fresh in his mind.

When the truck's air conditioner broke down, the agent

wouldn't stop to have it repaired; it was too big a risk, he told them, and they could all get caught. But without the air circulating in the back of the truck, conditions became so unbearable that one of the immigrants died of suffocation during the trip.

'We knew they wouldn't stop the truck,' Lucky tells me. 'A lot of the boys on the truck were young – even I was young – so we could handle it. But sadly, one man died. He was from El Salvador.' His voice is low, heavy with regret.

Horrified and angered by the death of one of their fellow travellers on board, the men inside the truck created an uproar and demanded that they stop for some air. Finally, unable to pacify the immigrants, the agent halted the truck in a secluded cornfield and allowed everyone to get off so they could breathe in some fresh air.

'It had been three days in the trailer and when we saw the sunlight after so long, our eyes were blinded. They couldn't adjust when we finally saw light again.'

Lucky would stay back in Mexico until arrangements could be made for him to cross the border. It was a month before his agent gave him the next set of instructions; he was to board a bus that would take him across the border into Arizona. He would finally be in America.

From Arizona, Lucky called 'Bhaji', the owner of the restaurant in DC, to notify him that he had finally arrived. Then he paid the agent a final sum of money to arrange for his plane ticket from Arizona to the East Coast.

Airport security was far more relaxed in those pre-9/11 days and Lucky managed to board his flight without having to show the authorities any papers. When his flight landed in Baltimore, Bhaji was there at the airport to pick him up and drive him down to what would become his hometown in America – Washington, DC.

Lucky ended up paying the agent a total of '*sade saath* lakh *rupaiyah* [₹7,50,000]' for his trip to America as an undocumented immigrant.

'That's nothing,' he says in retrospect, dismissing his travails, and proceeds to tell us about a young man from Punjab who had paid his agent a sum of ₹45,00,000 for the same journey, only to be apprehended by the authorities in Mexico. Lucky would come to know later that the man had somehow made his way to California.

'I don't know if he's still in America,' he now muses. 'I never heard from him again.'

The Punjab-based agent whose services Lucky had used was well known for his expertise in helping to transport boys from the state to America without any legal documentation. So much so that the man had been on Interpol's radar for a while. He would eventually be apprehended in Costa Rica and taken into custody.

'He's in jail now, for 19 years, I've heard,' Lucky says, shaking his head as he stares out of the car window.

As we continue to chat, it is clear to me that the real price he paid in undertaking his journey to America was missing out on the birth of his only child.

'This is something that I can't get over,' he says with regret. 'And now my son is 18 years old. I still haven't seen him. He was born when I was in Costa Rica. Now my son is even taller than me. He is studying Defence Engineering. I haven't met him in person, but I talk to him every day.'

Shortly after he arrived in America, Lucky had to go through the experience of his first day at work. At the time, the man he calls Bhaji used to be a manager at a Blimpie sandwich shop in the city and it was he who had arranged for a job for Lucky that required him to work in the kitchen.

'When I arrived at nine in the morning for my first day of work, I was handed a huge bag of onions and told to slice them,' Lucky remembers. 'That day, I cried. I thought, where have I ended up?

'I thought about my dad immediately and how he never let me work when I was growing up. He only wanted me to focus on studying. I thought I would have been so much better off if I had stayed at home with him. But it was too late; I couldn't do anything about my situation.'

Listening to him, I couldn't help musing: this is how 'the craze to immigrate', especially illegally, can strip you of your identity. Whether you're well-educated or belong to a 'good family' is of little consequence – your entire background is erased the moment you enter a country where your reputation and credentials don't precede you. I've seen this happen time and again – the engineering major turned taxi driver, the law-school student making do as a Blimpie sandwich maker, the economics major reduced to the role of an unemployed housewife...

Lucky had not only completed university, but had held a number of jobs in India.

'When it came to studying, I was an intelligent pupil in school. I got good marks,' he recalls.

After graduation, his two closest friends would pursue legal studies and obtain law degrees. Unable to pay the fees for law school, Lucky could not keep up with them and inevitably, fell behind. 'Now both of my friends are attorneys in Chandigarh's High Court,' he says, repeating, 'the High Court!' for emphasis. 'They come over to see my mother, sometimes, and they tell her that I made the biggest mistake. "He was smart enough to continue studying," they say, "but look at him now; it's been eighteen years and he hasn't returned home to India."'

Thanks to Facebook and other social media, Lucky has been able to stay in touch with those friends and others back in India.

'I speak to them, sometimes, and they say, "Look at us; we've become attorneys. You could have too. You made a big mistake."'

For Lucky, it is obvious that the question of who he could have become, if he had stayed on in India, haunts him. But his lowest point came nearly 10 years after he had been living and working in the country. Having entered America as an undocumented immigrant, he had been trying for years to find a legal remedy to legitimize his status and had been working with immigration lawyers on his case to obtain a Green Card that would make him a legal resident. There had been no progress on his case for weeks, months and years.

Finally, after years of delay, he was granted an immigration-related interview.

'At the time, my father was ill,' he now recalls. 'My interview was at nine-thirty a.m. and at ten, when I came out, I called him to tell him that my interview was over and that my Green Card was in the process of being finalized. I spoke to my father at ten in the morning – it must have been around seven-thirty or eight in the evening back in India. That very night, just five hours later, my dad passed away.'

Lucky's father had sensed that he wouldn't be seeing his son again. Before he died, he wrote a message for his dear '*beta*' on a wall of his room that he was leaving this world, contented with the life he had lived, but his feelings were tinged with sadness at not being able to see his son one final time before his departure.

'My mother has saved that message and she says, "*Puttar* [son], when you come back home, you can see it on the wall and it'll be like you saw your dad before he left." That's been the most difficult time for me. I can't forget that. At the time, I was crying a lot, thinking, what have I done, why am I here?

'At that time, I really regretted coming to America and I

thought I shouldn't have come here at all. In India, I had been struggling too. I had been working at legal jobs. I was making decent money, but I had always been driven by the craze to come to America. When Dad passed away, I really thought, "Where have I ended up? Why am I here?"

'Then my mom helped me and gave me confidence. She told me that what was lost was lost, but I should keep working on what I have. "Come back here once you're successful, once you've achieved what you set out to do," she advised me.

'At that time, I thought I was just going to go back to India. But Bhaji and the others, they helped me get through it and persuaded me to stay. They told me, "Your life might feel ruined, but at least stay and work to build a life for your son back home." He's the reason why I stayed here, so I can provide a good life for him. And for my wife. It had been hardly five months since we were married. Now it's been 18 years since I last saw her.'

Lucky has yet to see it, but when he returns to India, the writing will still be on the wall in his father's room.

In the nearly 20 years that he has been in America, his life has become easier. Years of working in restaurant kitchens have taught him the fundamentals of running a successful food business. But along with picking up the tricks of preparing a good American meal, he has also imbibed the local culture and become fluent in both English and Spanish.

'In one of the restaurants,' he says, 'there was a Spanish boy who worked with me and a Spanish girl. I learned from them. They couldn't speak English and we couldn't speak Spanish. So we all kind of learned from an English-to-Spanish translation book. We all worked together.'

As the owner and manager of his food-truck business, Lucky serves up American food to his customers. A vegetarian himself, he's never tasted meat, but knows how to cook it to suit the American palate and serve it in the expected manner. For him, the biggest benefit of owning the business is the freedom it allows him to manage his own schedule. No longer needing to slave day and night in restaurant kitchens, he can finally work a Monday-to-Friday daytime schedule. And for that, Lucky is very grateful.

'I'm happier now that I don't have to work for anyone any more, that I have my own business,' he says. 'I can take a day off whenever I want.'

Every afternoon when he returns home, the first thing he does is check the mailbox. After spending countless hours with immigration lawyers and submitting one document after another, Lucky is confident that his legal permit – his Green Card – will arrive. He regards it as his ticket to further freedom, for it will allow him to finally make a trip back to India. He checks his mailbox every day with the same yearning with which he had looked forward as a young man to the chance of making his journey to America.

When I ask Lucky what he misses most about

his home country, he offers a simple, one-word reply: 'India.'

He goes on to explain what he means. 'India, it's all about the effect it has on the mind; it's a place of no stress,' he tells me. 'Let me tell you a story: we have a friend, he's a taxi driver in the city. He's an American citizen, his kids are citizens. He went to India in October and he hasn't come back since. When I call him to ask when he's coming back, he says, "Why do you keep calling me back to America? What's in your America that is so worthwhile for me to come back to? I've been in India since October and I haven't yet taken a pill for a headache. When I approach Dulles Airport, I know I'll start to feel the stress again. I know that as soon as I get back to the house, there will be a pile of bills waiting for me and I'll need to start working right away to pay them off. Sometimes, the taxi work is slow and that is so stressful, because you think, how will I pay the bills if work is slow?"'

I understand his friend's dilemma perfectly. I know this story well. Watching my father work for decades as a taxi driver, I have come to know which months in the year the taxi driving business is slow – August, when the city empties out for the summer holidays and even Congress is in recess; and December, when the city goes quiet again for Christmas. Those months can be crippling for taxi drivers who are accustomed to bringing home daily salaries. I know how stressful those days were for my father; I am also aware of how much he longs for a break from work.

Whether life in India is truly less stressful than it is abroad is debatable. But for Lucky, who hasn't returned home in decades, India is a place where he can finally take a break from work. America offers the capitalist's dream, the opportunity to work 24 hours a day and earn your way to prosperity. But it is most certainly not a place where you can enjoy a well-earned rest. Since moving to this country, Lucky has worked relentlessly and sent nearly a crore of rupees – about US $160,000 – back to India.

He speaks to his son almost daily over FaceTime and listens to him, as the boy assures him that once his own studies are complete, his father can retire.

'My son always says to me, "You've struggled so much, worked so hard... Once my university [course] is over, you can retire."

'When my son is all set, I want to go back,' Lucky goes on. 'I have made a beautiful house back in India and I've saved a little bit of money. I want to spend the last part of my life with my wife. I want us to enjoy our life together.'

I mull over his words. While he is, at the moment, driven by the desire to pack up and return to India as soon as his son completes his university studies, I wonder if that will really happen. I ponder over the possibility of him bringing his wife and son over to America, instead. For this is where Lucky has built a successful business and set up a home. His son has apparently told him that he will settle wherever his father chooses to live.

When I bring up the possibility of his family moving to America, Lucky says, 'If he comes here to America, he'll forget me. There's something in America's water, America *da paani*, that makes people forget about their parents. They don't take care of their parents here.'

His words sting. I wonder if that was an intentional jab directed at me – I had told him about leaving my parents in this country and moving to the UK. Or perhaps, he's overcome by guilt for having left his own parents back in India when he chose to move to America?

'As soon as I get my Green Card, I'm going to India,' he declares.

As I will learn later, that's exactly what he does. The day his legal papers come through in the mail, Lucky buys a return ticket to India. At the time I am busy writing his story, he is visiting the place of his birth, reuniting with his mother, wife and son. But, he plans to return to the US and bring his wife and son along with him one day. For now, at least, America will continue to be home.

Notes

[1] Due to the sensitive nature of his situation, this interviewee's name has been changed.

[2] Zavis, Alexandra, 'Haitians, Africans, Asians', *LA Times*, 22 December 2016.

Acknowledgements

With immense gratitude, I thank the many people around the world who have opened up their homes to me and shared with me their life stories. The kindness and generosity I've received over the years of writing this book is something I will always cherish, and I'm grateful for the new friends I've made across the thriving global network of Indians abroad.

Truly, this book would not have been possible without the support and dedication of Kanishka Gupta. I am forever thankful to you.

A sincere thank you to my editors, Prerna and Mita, who have worked tirelessly to bring these stories to life.

A special thanks to my mother- and father-in-law, Pratibha and Naresh, who encouraged me to finish when I was ready to give up. And to my parents, Jagtej and Varinder, who I miss every moment of every day – you are my strength and my luck, and I will forever need your guiding light.

And, Prit. Thank you for sharing every step of this journey with me, yet another adventure in our story.